To Doug :
Wish you healthy
and happy eating !
Lily Loh
1995

↑ Pan-fried Shrimp Dumplings (page 76)

↓ Sizzling Rice Soup (page 92)

↑ Shredded Daikon with Cilantro (page 102)

↓ Steamed Flower-shaped Prawns (page 142)

↑ Miniature Shrimp Pears (page 77)

↓ Menu #18 (page 59)

↑ Sweet & Sour Shrimp (page 135)

↓ Fresh Asparagus Salad (page 101)

↑ Sauteed Tofu, Family Style (page 158)

↓ Menu #7 (page 55)

↑ Baked Savory Tofu with Spinach (page 156)

↓ Fish Fillets with Oyster Sauce (page 123)

↑ Snow Peas with Mushrooms and Bamboo Shoots (page 171)

↓ Braised Tofu with Ham (page 161)

↑ Crispy Fish on Toast (page 73)

↓ Three Exotic Fruits on Crushed Ice (page 186)

Lily Loh's Chinese Seafood & Vegetables

by Lily Loh, C.C.P.

Introduction by **MARTIN YAN**
Chinese chef, teacher, and author

Forward by **HELEN TSOU, R.D.**

Edited by **AMY ADDISON-LICAMELI**

Illustrated by **CAROL HSIUNG LIU**

Photography by **GEORGE LOH**

SOLANA PUBLISHING COMPANY
California

LILY LOH'S
CHINESE SEAFOOD & VEGETABLES

Copyright © 1991 by Lily Loh

All rights reserved

Library of Congress Cataloging - in - Publication data

Loh, Lily.
 Lily Loh's Chinese Seafood & Vegetables.
 Includes index.
 1. Cookery, Chinese. 2. Seafood. 3. Vegetables. I. Title.
TX724.5L69   1991   641.5951   91-90564

ISBN: Hardcover: 0-9630299-0-8

Typesetting by Alpha & Ωmega Typesetting, Oceanside, California
Printed by Mei Ching Publishing Co., Taiwan
Published by Solana Publishing Co., California

FIRST EDITION

DEDICATION

*to my **parents***
for my education

*to my **family***
for their support

*to my **friends***
for their encouragement

Yan Can & Company

INTRODUCTION

Seafood, particularly fish, is a very popular ingredient in Chinese cooking. For the Chinese, fresh fish means that it was most likely swimming just minutes before it was cooked. When I came to this country, I discovered that America had plenty of seafood available. But the fish came in many different forms . . . canned, frozen, breaded. As I teach and talk to students around the country, I have found that they are very concerned with their health and know that fish can be a healthy menu item...but they do not use much fresh fish. Why? Because they are not sure how to buy it, how to store it, and most of all how to prepare it.

In this book, my good friend Lily, has not only given the reader, many wonderful and delicious recipes for using fish and seafood, but she has included everything you need to know to handle these ingredients properly. With this book you can have nutritious and tasty meals just as you have enjoyed them in many Chinese restaurants. I am sure you will find these recipes equally enjoyable.

Besides fish and shellfish, Lily has compiled many wonderful vegetable, soup, and tofu recipes. The chapters on how to plan a Chinese meal, how to use chopsticks, and how to use other typical Chinese ingredients will guide you to prepare many authentic and healthy Chinese meals.

Martin Yan
Host of Yan Can Cook Show

FOREWORD

Mrs. Lily Loh has been teaching Chinese cuisine for fifteen years in California. Her classes range from beginning to advanced Chinese cooking.

Born in China, Lily is a graduate of Cornell University where she majored in Home Economics. The combination of being native to the cuisine and her vast experience in teaching Americans, in addition to her educational background, has resulted in a cookbook that is unique in its field. Unlike other Chinese cookbooks which are more comprehensive in nature, this volume is unique in that it specializes in seafood and other recipes with the goal of providing good nutrition as well as good-tasting food. By anticipating the needs of American cooks, she has produced a "user friendly" Chinese cookbook with numerous easy to follow menus, step-by-step instructions, while simultaneously stressing the importance of nutrition in relation to health. These valuable features help the cook to organize and save time; they also make a complex cuisine simple and easily attainable by any Chinese food aficionado and by all those who seek wellness as well as enjoyment of good cooking.

To promote optimum health, dietitians today are more than ever urging people to reduce their intake of red meat and to incorporate into their diet more fish and other seafood, vegetables and fruits, and other food groups rich in complex carbohydrates. The Chinese people have always eaten this way, as reflected by their menus and recipes. The fact that Chinese cuisine is also one of the most delicious in the world is responsible for its unprecedented and continuing popularity in this country.

I congratulate Lily for writing this timely volume which is a testimonial to her love of people and the desire to share her expertise, and I heartily recommend it to health-conscious Americans and Chinese cooking enthusiasts everywhere.

Helen Tsou R.D.

Helen Tsou
Registered Dietitian
West Los Angeles VA Medical Center
Los Angeles, California

ACKNOWLEDGEMENTS

My students have been requesting that I write a Chinese cookbook since I began to teach fifteen years ago. I have finally decided to write down all my students' and my family's favorite dishes in this book in the hopes that more people will enjoy the delicious and healthy way of eating Chinese food. I am grateful to all my students for their encouragement.

A special thanks to my colleague, Carole Bloom, who telephoned me every month to see how I was getting along with my cookbook. Without her coaching, I might still be at the drawing board today. I am also grateful that she introduced me to Kitty Morse, Pamela Wischkaemper, and Betz Collins who have given me invaluable suggestions.

My thanks to Amy Han, who encouraged me to teach cooking when we first moved to California and suggested that I write a cookbook; to Norwin Clark, who spent hours in the kitchen testing and retesting my recipes; to Clara Norris for her expertise in typing and Kati Bower, owner of Alpha & Ωmega Typesetting, for her expert typesetting. Without them this book would never have been completed.

The beautiful dishes in the pictures were borrowed from my good friends Marta Maria Pumpelly, Ginger Gaubert, Norma Morris, and Anne Dvorak. I am thankful for having such wonderful friends, who not only trusted me with their precious dishes, but also have been so enthusiastic about my cookbook.

I am so fortunate to have Carol Hsiung Liu to be this book's illustrator. She is not only an artist but also has a degree in Architecture from Cornell University, my old alma mater. Her artistic drawings are priceless because they were done with so much love and creativity.

To my editor, Amy Addison-Licameli, who has put her whole heart into working on my book, I am forever grateful. Without her expert knowledge of cookbooks, I would still be struggling. Words cannot express how much I appreciate my friends who helped me with my manuscript. Jackie Eginton, Jan Cantwell, and Kathryn Krammer are just a few who have read and reread my drafts. They have spent hours making corrections and suggestions.

Finally, I would like to thank especially my mother-in-law, Grace Loh, from whom I have learned many of my culinary skills; my grandfather-in-law, T. P. Lin, who has given me many Chinese cookbooks and much inspiration; my sisters and brothers, who are so helpful and encouraging; my mother, who has taught me the joy of cooking; and my father, who has written all the beautiful Chinese characters in this book and is a continuing inspiration for me.

Last, but not the least, a million thanks to my children and my husband who have sampled and evaluated every dish in this cookbook. My daughter, Christina, has been most supportive. My son, Derek, is my ultimate taster. If he likes a dish, then I know everyone will love it. George, my husband, who has been my friend and companion for the past 23 years, is invaluable to my career. He has not only helped me every step towards creating this book but also spent every Saturday for the past year taking photographs to illustrate my cookbook. Without him, I know that "Lily Loh's Chinese Seafood & Vegetables" would never have been printed.

CONTENTS

Contents (Continued)

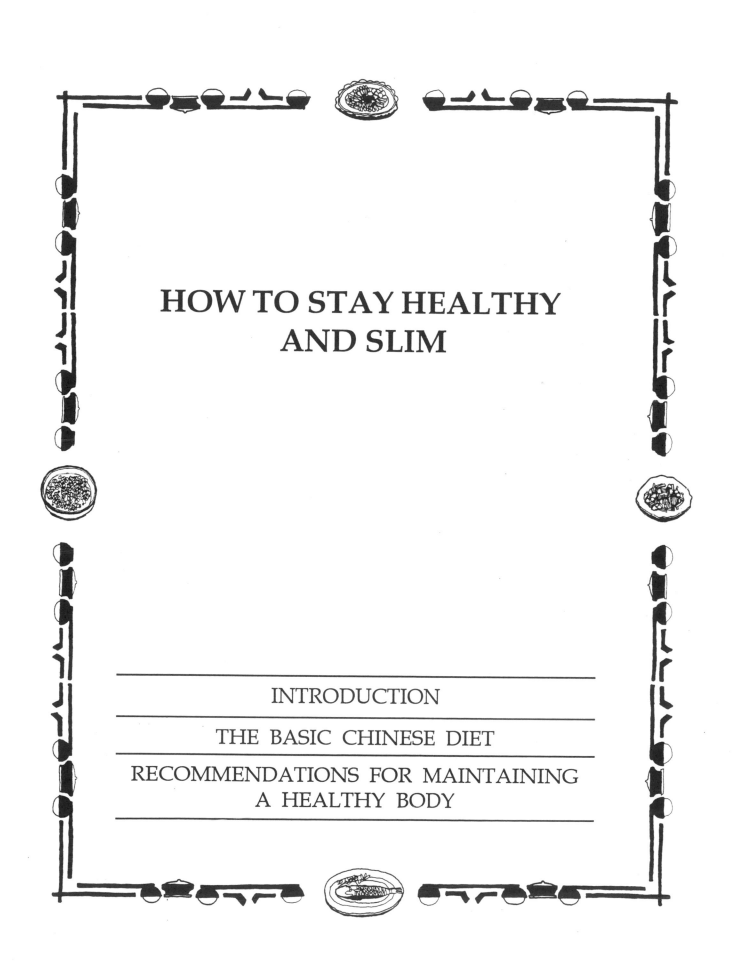

HOW TO STAY HEALTHY AND SLIM

INTRODUCTION

THE BASIC CHINESE DIET

RECOMMENDATIONS FOR MAINTAINING
A HEALTHY BODY

HOW TO STAY HEALTHY AND SLIM

INTRODUCTION

The Chinese way of eating promotes good health and longer life according to a diet study by Dr. T. Colin Campbell, a nutritional biochemist at Cornell University. This is because it consists mainly of vegetables and grains. According to Dr. Campbell, Chinese consume 20% more calories than Americans, and yet, are 25% leaner. One of the reasons is that Chinese eat only a third of the amount of fat Americans do, while they consume twice the starch and vegetables.

There are few overweight people in China. Diet pills and crash diets are almost unknown. In fact, there is an old saying: "If a wife gains weight, her husband must be on the road to success." In China, it is considered a compliment to tell a lady "You look like you have gained some weight." That is because the Chinese diet is so low in fat that the Chinese generally do not gain weight easily.

THE BASIC CHINESE DIET

The basic Chinese diet consists primarily of grains, seafood, fresh vegetables, and fruits. Meat is served sparingly. The Chinese get 80% of their calories from grains. The remaining 20% of the calories are from vegetables, fruits, and protein foods. Garbage cans in Chinese parks are often called "fruit peel containers." The Chinese enjoy fresh fruits for between meal snacks as well as mealtime desserts. Seafood and tofu, major sources of protein, are served daily. Both are low in fat and calories. Seafood, especially white fish, has much less cholesterol than beef. See the following chart:

CHOLESTEROL IN FOODS*		
	Cholesterol In Milligrams	
Fruits, grains, vegetables, tofu	0	LOW
Oysters (cooked, about 3½ oz.)	45	
Scallops (cooked, about 3½ oz.)	53	
Clams (cooked, about 3½ oz.)	65	
Fish, lean (cooked, about 3½ oz.)	65	
Chicken/Turkey, light meat (without skin) (cooked, about 3½ oz.)	80	
Lobster (cooked, about 3½ oz.)	85	
Beef, lean (cooked, about 3½ oz.)	90	
Chicken/Turkey, dark meat (without skin) (cooked, about 3½ oz.)	95	
Crab (cooked, about 3½ oz.)	100	
Shrimp (cooked, about 3½ oz.)	150	
Egg yolk, one	270	
Beef Liver (cooked, about 3½ oz.)	440	
Beef Kidney (cooked, about 3½ oz.)	700	HIGH

*Chart from USDA publication.

According to the latest research from the American Heart Association, one of the greatest risk factors for developing hardening of the arteries is a high level of blood cholesterol. There are two ways people develop high cholesterol: 1. by high cholesterol intake, and 2. by consuming food high in saturated fat, from which our bodies make cholesterol.

Too much fat in the diet also leads to increased risk of breast, prostrate and colon/rectal cancer. There is an interesting article on a recent discovery by the American Institute for Cancer Research. They have found that Asian women have five times less breast cancer than American women. The presence of isoflavones in tofu, which Asians consume in quantity, act as a natural block in the development of breast cancer.

One good reason Chinese people have fewer heart diseases is because butter is never served or used in cooking. Vegetable oil, corn oil, and peanut oil are used to stir-fry and deep-fry food in China. By looking at the chart below, you can see why the Chinese way of cooking is healthier:

OILS AND FATS*		
Type of Oil or Fat	Percent Polyunsaturated Fat	Percent Saturated Fat
Canola Oil	31%	6%
Safflower Oil	74%	9%
Sunflower Oil	64%	10%
Corn Oil	58%	13%
Average Vegetable Oil	40%	13%
Peanut Oil	30%	19%
Chicken Fat	26%	29%
Olive Oil	9%	14%
Average Vegetable Shortening	20%	32%
Lard	12%	40%
Beef Fat	4%	48%
Butter	4%	61%
Palm Oil	2%	81%
Coconut Oil	2%	86%

*Chart from USDA publication.

Canola oil has the lowest saturated fat. This is the oil that my family uses for all types of cooking. It is made from rape seed, which comes from the mustard seed family, now grown mainly in Canada. Another popular oil that the Chinese use is corn oil, which has 58% polyunsaturated fat and 13% saturated fat. Compared to butter, which has only 4% polyunsaturated fat but 61% saturated fat, the vegetable oils are far better for you. Palm oil and coconut oil, which are found in many western food products, are not used by the Chinese. Both of these types of oil are high in saturated fat.

Cheese and cream are not a part of the Chinese daily diet. Both of these ingredients are high in fat and calories. The Chinese get calcium from tofu and tofu products. In the chart below, compare the grams of fat in dairy products; for instance ice cream versus tofu.

Food	Amount	Calcium (Milligrams)	Fat (Grams)
CALCIUM AND FAT CONTENT OF COMMON FOODS*			
Milk and Dairy Products			
American Cheese	1 oz.	174 mg.	8.9 g.
Cottage Cheese, creamed	1 cup	126 mg.	9.5 g.
Ice Cream, hard	1 cup	176 mg.	14.3 g.
Lowfat Milk (2%)	1 cup	297 mg.	4.7 g.
Green Leafy Vegetables			
Broccoli, cooked	1 cup	178 mg.	0.4 g.
Spinach, cooked	1 cup	244 mg.	0.5 g.
Other Vegetables			
Beans, green snap, cooked	1 cup	58 mg.	0.4 g.
Soybeans, cooked	½ cup	131 mg.	5.8 g.
Sweet Potato, baked in skin	1 small	40 mg.	0.5 g.
Nuts			
Almonds, roasted and salted	¼ cup	92 mg.	22.6 g.
Sesame Seeds, dried, hulled	¼ cup	40 mg.	17.6 g.
Seafood			
Scallops, steamed	3½ oz.	115 mg.	1.4 g.
Shrimp, raw	3½ oz.	63 mg.	0.8 g.
Salmon, canned	3½ oz.	249 mg.	5.2 g.
Other Foods			
Bread, white or whole wheat	2 slices	46 mg.	2.0 g.
Cream of Celery Soup, made with milk	1 serving	135 mg.	33.0 g.
Orange, raw	1 medium	56 mg.	0.1 g.
Tofu	4 oz.	154 mg.	5.0 g.

*Chart from USDA publication.

The basic Chinese diet is also high in complex carbohydrates and fiber. Rice, noodles, beans, legumes, fresh vegetables, and fruits make up a major part of a typical Chinese meal. Rice and noodles are cooked in plain water without butter or salt. Fresh vegetables are never overcooked. Fruit is eaten raw without glazes of honey, chocolate, or rich sauce. Desserts, like cakes and cookies, are only served on special occasions. The Chinese do not crave sweet desserts because a small amount of sugar is used in their cooking.

Salt is not a table condiment. Neither is it a Chinese practice to pour soy sauce on rice or other foods at the table. The cook seasons the food before it is served. Soy sauce has less sodium than salt. Two tablespoons of medium soy sauce is equivalent, in sodium content, to one teaspoon of salt. Rice also contains less sodium than bread per serving.

RECOMMENDATIONS FOR MAINTAINING A HEALTHY BODY

The U.S. Department of Health and Human Services recommends the following:

1. **Eat a variety of foods** — There are over 80,000 Chinese recipes, each with ingredients rich in a variety of vitamins and nutrients.

2. **Maintain a desirable weight** — You should weigh within your ideal body weight. Most Chinese do.

3. **Avoid excess fat, saturated fat, and cholesterol** — Eat more seafood and tofu in place of meat and cheese. Cook with vegetable oil instead of butter and saturated fats.

4. **Avoid too much sodium and sugar** — Season lightly as you cook. Do not add extra salt at the table. Consume less sweets and desserts; eat more fresh fruits instead.

5. **Increase starch and fiber** — Eat more rice or noodles, beans and fresh vegetables daily.

6. **If you drink alcoholic beverages, do so in moderation** — Alcoholic beverages are high in calories and low in nutrients. Drink soup and tea instead.

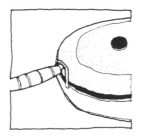

HOW TO SERVE AND EAT
A CHINESE MEAL

HOW TO SERVE AND EAT A CHINESE MEAL

HOW TO SERVE A CHINESE MEAL

Most Westerners are surprised to learn that the Chinese do not use large dinner plates. Our basic tableware includes:

1. Rice bowl and soup bowl

2. Small plate — about 5 to 6 inches in diameter

3. Chopsticks and spoon

4. Small tea cup

The rice bowl is held in one hand and the chopsticks in the other. The Chinese do not fill their plates with food before starting to eat. Instead, everyone serves and eats at the same time. Small amounts of food are placed on the rice or on the small plate. Some families use serving spoons while others turn their chopsticks around to serve with the clean ends. Seating diners at a round table is the easiest way to serve a Chinese meal. The food is within reach of everyone so it does not have to be passed.

For breakfast, the Eastern and the Southern Chinese eat congee. Congee is rice cooked with a lot of water, much like porridge. Small pickles, salted fish, roasted peanuts, and eggs are served with congee. The Northern Chinese like to have a tofu drink with steamed bread and dumplings in the morning.

Lunch and dinner are often similar, as both are important meals. Now that more people work outside the home, lunch has been simpler. Fried rice or noodle dishes are often served for lunch.

HOW TO SERVE A FORMAL DINNER

Eating is extremely important in China. as illustrated by this old saying, "The Chinese live to eat." Every important occasion is celebrated with an elaborate banquet.

For a formal dinner, the complete table setting is shown below:

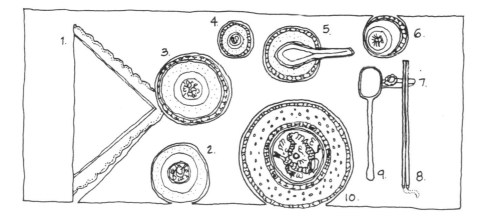

1. Napkin	6. Tea Cup
2. Dessert Bowl	7. Chopstick Rest
3. Rice Bowl	8. Chopsticks
4. Sauce Dish	9. Serving Spoon
5. Spoon Dish and Soup Spoon	10. Serving Dish

A Lazy Susan is often placed in the center of a large round table to facilitate serving. The guest of honor is always seated at the head of the table, which is the seat facing the front door. In China, the oldest person is highly respected. Usually he or she is seated at the head. A banquet often lasts two or three hours with a minimum of ten courses. If you ever get invited to a Chinese banquet, remember to pace yourself. Each dish is served as a separate course. Do not overeat at the beginning for the best dishes are always served at the end!

DIFFERENT TYPES OF CHINESE FOOD

There are five main regional foods in China:

1. *Cantonese* - Southern

2. *Szechuanese* (Sichuanese) - Western

3. *Mandarin* - Northern

4. *Hunanese* - Central

5. *Shanghainese* - Eastern

MAP OF CHINA

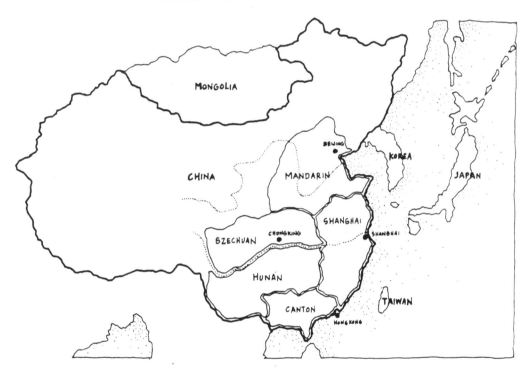

The Cantonese are seafarers and were the first to establish restaurants outside of China. This is the reason Cantonese dishes are so popular among the Westerners. Since Canton is located on the ocean, the Cantonese are famous for seafood, especially lobster and fish. Many Cantonese dishes are stir-fried and seasoned with rich oyster sauce and fermented black beans. Barbecued Pork, Spare Ribs and Roast Duck are also specialties from this region.

In Canton and Hong Kong, one can go to a tea house and enjoy Dim Sum. The word "Dim Sum" means "Heart's Pleasure." An array of little steamed dumplings, sweets and pastries are served on push carts. The Cantonese are experts in making each tiny dish taste scrumptious.

Szechuan food is extremely hot and spicy. Because refrigeration is still rare in China, the Szechuanese cook with lots of red chili peppers and many different spices in order to preserve food. A popular Szechuan dish is Kung Pao Chicken—diced chicken cooked with dry red peppers and peanuts. Dry Shredded Beef and Szechuan Pickles are also well known dishes from this area.

Most people associate Mandarin food—the cuisine of Northern China—with the most elegant and delicate of Chinese cooking. Since Beijing is the capital of China, formal dinners are frequently served in this part of the country. The most famous banquet dish is Peking Duck served with paper thin pancakes and hoisin sauce or plum sauce. Mo Shu Pork is a poor man's substitute for this duck dish.

The climate in northern China is extremely cold in the winters and hot in the summers. Therefore, the main diet staple is not rice but wheat flour. Noodles and steamed breads are served more often than rice. Because this diet is so different from the rest of China, the people are bigger and stronger than in other Chinese provinces.

Hunanese food is authentically Chinese and not as spicy as Szechuan, yet not as mild as Mandarin. This central region of China is seldom visited by Westerners. Since the Hunan Province is located near the Yantse River, many fresh-water fish dishes, such as Steamed Carp andSmoked Yellow Fish, have originated in this area. Other favorite Hunan dishes include Honey Glazed Ham and Steamed Minced Pigeon Soup in Bamboo Cup. If you ever eat in a Hunanese restaurant, make sure to order these two dishes. You will not be disappointed.

Since I was born in Shanghai, I grew up with the dishes from this region. My family really enjoys fish, chicken, pork, beef, or duck cooked in a rich dark soy sauce with rock candy. This sauce is often called "The Master Sauce" and can be used over and over again. Rice is served with every meal. Most Shanghainese dishes have a wonderful sauce to go with the aromatic rice.

HOW TO EAT WITH CHOPSTICKS

The Chinese learn how to eat with chopsticks when very young, around 3 or 4 years old. Before this age, a spoon is used. The most enjoyable way to eat Chinese food is with chopsticks which allows one to select and savor each bite.

Dining etiquette in China is much different from that of the Western world. A knife is never placed on the table. This is considered barbaric. Because chopsticks are an extension of one's fingers, it is proper to hold food to the mouth and bite off pieces. To eat the Chinese way, hold the rice bowl in one hand and use the chopsticks to scoop or shovel the rice into your mouth. This is easier than trying to pick up individual clusters of rice. Practice and soon you'll enjoy eating with chopsticks.

As a rule, the top ends of the chopsticks are square and the bottom ends are round. Use the rounded ends for eating and the square ends for serving. Always hold chopsticks a little above the mid-point. Do not hold chopsticks too low or you will not be able to open and close them easily. However, if you hold them too high, you will not have as much control either.

Three easy steps for using chopsticks are as follows:

1. Extend one chopstick about 3 inches beyond the end of the ring finger. Rest the upper half of the chopstick in the curve between the thumb and the index finger.

2. Hold the second chopstick between the thumb, index finger and middle finger.

3. Move the second chopstick up and down, keeping the tips even. Use the chopsticks to scoop rather than pick up each bite individually. Now relax and enjoy your meal.

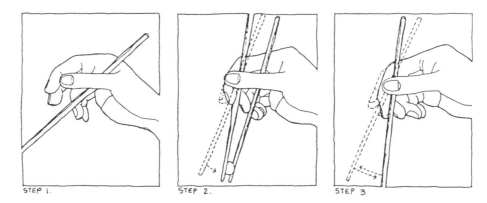

STEP 1.   STEP 2.   STEP 3.

DIFFERENT TYPES OF CHOPSTICKS

There are many different types of chopsticks on the market. Disposable ones are used in most restaurants. They are wrapped in paper. You may need to separate them yourself. Since this kind of chopsticks is not well polished, remove any splinters by rubbing one stick against the other a few times. This will smooth out the rough edges.

The most common chopsticks are made of wood. They are inexpensive and sold in packages of 10. You can wash them in your dishwasher. Some dishwashers have a long vertical compartment perfect for chopsticks. If your machine does not have such a compartment, place the chopsticks on the top rack, but place a few cups on top to prevent them from floating during washing.

Chopsticks also come in plastic, ivory, and silver. The silver chopsticks are rare and are always chained at the end. The emperors used them to detect poison because silver turns black when it comes into contact with arsenic. Plastic and lacquered chopsticks are quite slippery. Use these only after you have mastered wooden ones. Ivory chopsticks are often given as birthday or wedding souvenirs to guests. Names and dates may be carved into them to commemorate the special occasion.

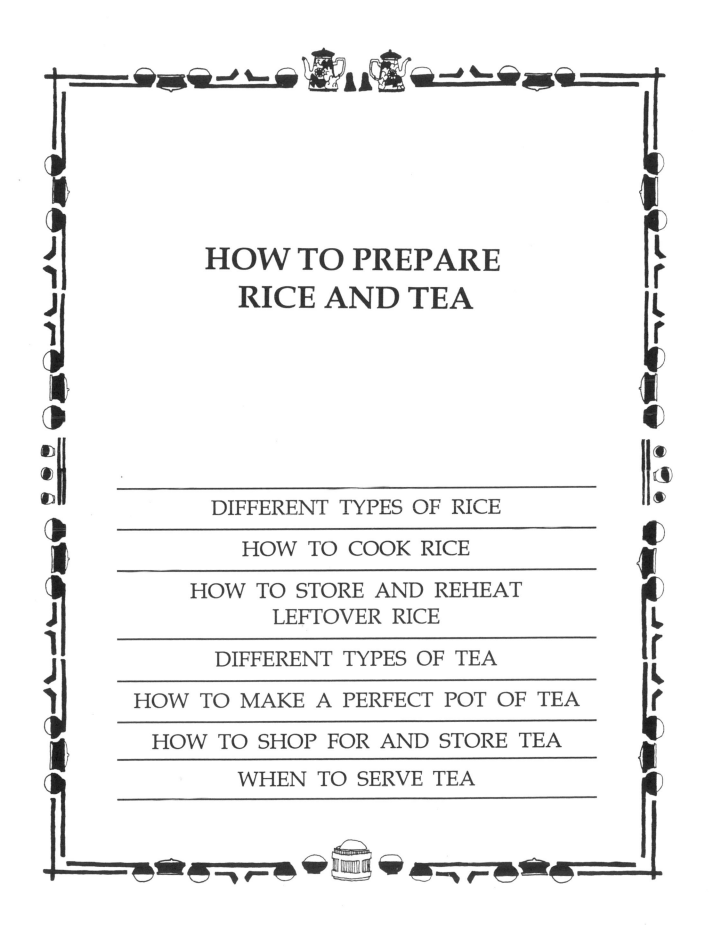

HOW TO PREPARE RICE AND TEA

DIFFERENT TYPES OF RICE

HOW TO COOK RICE

HOW TO STORE AND REHEAT
LEFTOVER RICE

DIFFERENT TYPES OF TEA

HOW TO MAKE A PERFECT POT OF TEA

HOW TO SHOP FOR AND STORE TEA

WHEN TO SERVE TEA

HOW TO PREPARE RICE AND TEA

DIFFERENT TYPES OF RICE

Rice is mild in flavor and goes well with Chinese food. It is an excellent source of complex carbohydrates, an important part of a healthy diet. In addition, rice is low in calories. A one-half cup serving of cooked rice contains 82 calories. Rice has only a trace of fat and is cholesterol free. It is also non-allergenic and low in sodium.

There are basically two types of white rice:

1. **Long grain** — slender and long in shape. When cooked, the grains tend to remain separate and are light and fluffy.

2. **Short grain** — round in shape. When cooked, the grains tend to cling together and have a delightful aroma.

Most Chinese prefer short grain white rice because it has more flavor and aroma. It is easier to eat with chopsticks since the grains tend to stick together.

Brown rice has only the hull removed. This rice is served mostly in the northern part of China where the main starch foods are noodles, steamed bread, and pancakes. Brown rice has a slightly chewy texture and a nut-like flavor. The light brown color of brown rice is caused by the presence of seven bran layers which are rich in minerals and vitamins, especially the B-complex group. When cooking brown rice, you need to add more water and allow more time for cooking.

HOW TO COOK RICE

There are several ways to cook rice:

1. **Rice Cooker** — This is the easiest and most common method to cook rice. Simply follow the manufacturer's instructions. A rice cooker steams rice, keeps it warm automatically, and cooks perfect rice every time.

2. **Microwave Oven** — Microwaving saves energy and clean up time. Combine water and rice in a microwave-proof baking dish. Cover and microwave on High for 5 minutes or until boiling. Reduce setting to Medium (50% power) and cook 15 minutes for white rice. For brown rice, reduce setting to Medium-low (30% power) and cook 45-55 minutes. Let the rice rest for 10 minutes. Fluff and serve.

3. **Top of the Range** — Follow the recipe below:

RICE

Serves 4   **Difficulty level 1**

Rice	Water	Cooking Time	Yield
1 Cup White Long Grain	1 3/4-2 Cups	15 Mins.	3 Cups
1 Cup White Short Grain	1 1/2 Cups	15 Mins.	3 Cups
1 Cup Brown	2-2 1/2 Cups	45-50 Mins.	3-4 Cups

1. To rinse rice, pour it into a heavy 2-quart sauce pan. Add enough cold water to cover completely and stir thoroughly. Drain rice. Add measured water and bring to a boil over high heat. (If rice is old — and therefore dry — add another 1/4 cup of water.) Boil for 2-3 minutes or until craterlike holes appear in surface of rice. Cover pan tightly, reduce heat to low and cook for 15 minutes. Turn off heat; leave pan covered. Let rice rest for 10 minutes.

2. Remove cover and fluff rice. Serve hot. If rice must wait, keep in a covered, heatproof serving bowl in a preheated 250°F oven.

HOW TO STORE AND REHEAT RICE

Leftover rice can be refrigerated and kept for a few days. Be sure to cover the container tightly so the grains will not dry out or absorb flavors from other foods.

To reheat leftover rice, resteam it in a rice cooker. Or, put rice in a colander and place in a large pot with 1" of boiling water. Cover pot and steam for 5 to 10 minutes—depending upon the amount of rice. In a microwave oven, add two tablespoons of water and cook 1 to 1½ minutes per cup, on High setting.

DIFFERENT TYPES OF TEA

All tea comes from the same plant in the Camellia family. This plant grows about waist high and has flowers like a camellia. Varieties of tea are created by the various processing methods of the leaves and by the specific conditions in which the plants have grown — locale, climate, and time of harvest. As with wine, these conditions affect the quality of the tea leaves. There are about 250 varieties of Chinese tea and their prices vary from a few cents to hundreds of dollars per pound.

Basically, there are two types of tea:

1. **Green Tea** — resembles the original leaves on the tea plant. It is unfermented and receives very little handling. The leaves are picked before they wither and are dried immediately, either in the sun or with currents of warm air in special drying rooms. The smaller and younger leaves are more expensive than the large, older ones. Green tea produces a pale golden brew and goes well with light, stir-fried food. It is popular in warm weather because green tea is very refreshing in flavor as well as in appearance.

2. **Black or Red Tea** — comes from leaves permitted to wither on the bush. These leaves are gathered, rolled, fermented, and dried. Fermentation causes the leaves to change color from green to brownish-black. Black tea produces a rich, red brew which is the reason Chinese call it red tea. It goes well with deep-fried and spicy food and is served mainly during cool weather.

Oolong tea is partly dried and partly fermented. This tea produces a deep amber brew with the rich aroma of black tea and the delicate fragrance of green tea. Oolong goes well with any meal, whether light or heavy. This is the most popular tea serve in restaurants. Jasmine tea is Oolong tea leaves mixed with Jasmine flowers. Most people think Jasmine is an herbal tea, but it is not.

Chrysanthemum is not a tea but an herbal flower. The flower has no caffeine and is a relaxant. Chrysanthemum is a perfect drink before bedtime. It is usually found with dry goods instead of with the teas. Be careful not to drink too much of the following herbal teas: catnip, chamomile, juniper, and marigold. Use these teas and many other herbal teas in moderation, for they have undesirable side effects.

The following chart from the American Dietetic Association shows the caffeine content in popular beverages:

CAFFEINE CONTENT OF BEVERAGES*	
Beverages	**Caffeine (Mg/100 Ml.)**
Dripolated Coffee	97.00
Instant Coffee	44.00
Black Tea, Bagged	33.00
Black Tea, Loose	29.00
Green Tea Leaves	25.00
Coca Cola	17.97

*Chart from USDA publication.

HOW TO MAKE A PERFECT POT OF TEA

To brew a perfect pot of tea, always use fresh water. Bring the water to a boil, but do not overboil. Too much oxygen will be lost, and the tea leaves will sink to the bottom at once and not steep properly. However, if the water is not hot enough, the tea leaves will float, and the cup of tea will be tasteless and weak.

Scald the teapot with boiling water first. Use 1/2 teaspoon of loose tea leaves per cup or 1/2 teaball per pot. Pour boiling water over the tea leaves and steep for a few minutes: one to two minutes for weak tea, five to six minutes for full-bodied. Loose tea leaves may be brewed more than once. In fact, the second pot is milder and more mellow than the first.

HOW TO SHOP FOR AND STORE TEA

When shopping for tea, buy loose tea leaves in canisters. Loose tea is generally better quality and the container keeps the tea fresh longer. Teas wrapped in foil are the next best buy. Keep wrapped teas in the freezer, away from air and light which stales tea quickly. I do not recommend buying tea bags which are usually less fresh and fragrant.

WHEN TO SERVE TEA

Tea is the beverage of China. It is served in the morning, at noon, and at night. Most Chinese drink tea at the end of meals, except the Cantonese, who like to have tea during meals. For banquets, tea is sipped throughout the meal to cleanse the palate between courses.

According to many Chinese physicians, drinking tea after meals assists fat breakdown and helps with digestion. Since tea is made with boiled water, having a cup of tea is a good way to add liquid to the diet without adding calories.

There are many symbolic customs associated with tea. For instance, when a guest arrives, tea is served as a gesture of hospitality. At business meetings, one is expected to leave after one finishes a pot of tea. On the first day after a wedding, the bride and the groom are expected to serve tea to their in-laws as a sign of filial piety. All these customs have developed to help make life more gracious and enjoyable.

茶能止渴 提神明目益思想

"Tea quenches the thirst, keeps one alert,
improves eyesight, and helps the thinking process."

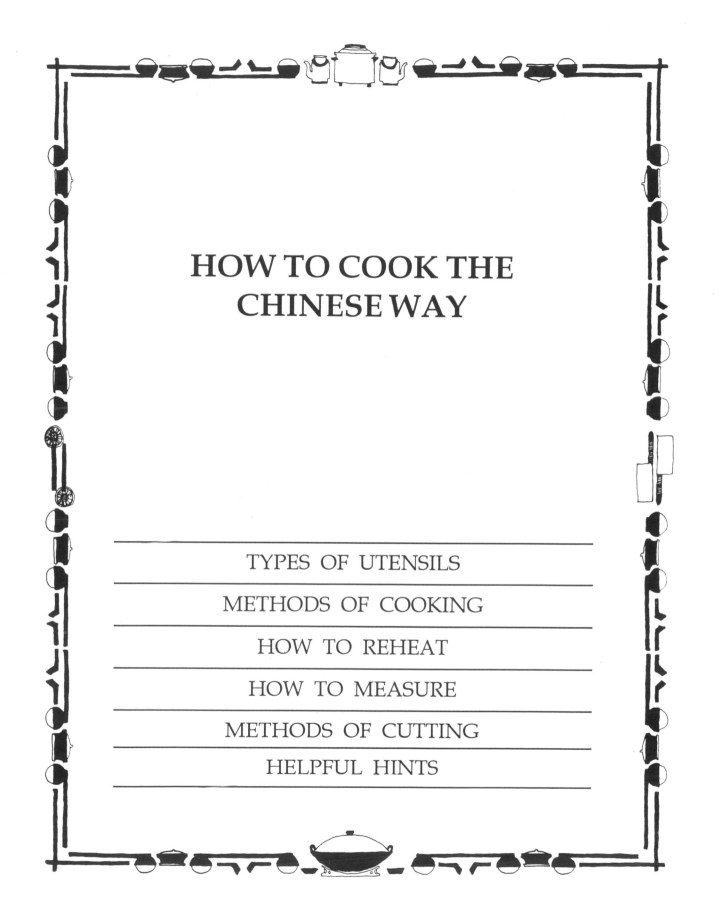

HOW TO COOK THE CHINESE WAY

TYPES OF UTENSILS

METHODS OF COOKING

HOW TO REHEAT

HOW TO MEASURE

METHODS OF CUTTING

HELPFUL HINTS

HOW TO COOK THE CHINESE WAY

TYPES OF UTENSILS

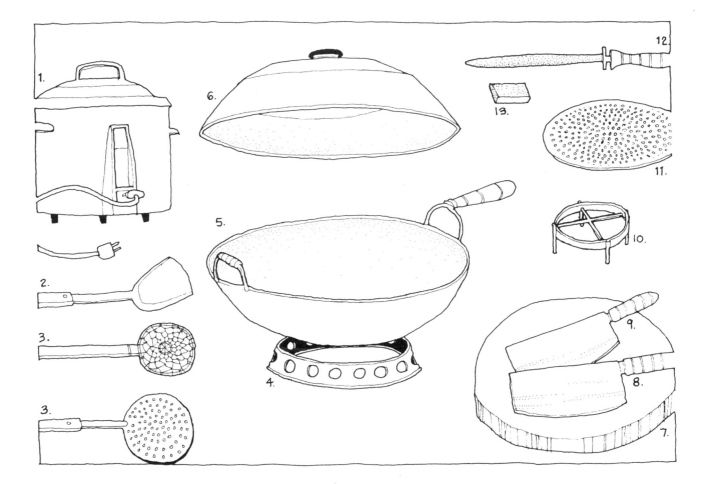

1. Rice Cooker	8. Cleaver (Chopper)
2. Spatula	9. Cleaver (Slicer)
3. Strainer	10. Steam Rack
4. Ring	11. Steam Plate
5. Wok	12. Sharpening Steel
6. Cover	13. Sharpening Stone
7. Cutting Board	

The wok is the most basic piece of cookware in Chinese cooking. You can cook Chinese food without a wok, but a wok is versatile and handy to have in any kitchen. Its round shape makes it easy to stir-fry, deep-fry, steam, and smoke.

The best wok to buy has one long wooden handle and one short wooden handle. Traditionally, woks were made of cast iron. Now they are also made of other metals. The most popular are made of carbon steel and are available in Chinese grocery stores. They are lighter than cast iron woks and rust less easily. The best way to prevent rusting is to use the wok often. To remove rust, soak in white vinegar.

Electric woks are not as practical as carbon steel woks. Most have a non-stick finish and thus are not recommended for use with high heat, nor for deep-frying, smoking, or steaming.

Season a new carbon steel wok before using.

INSTRUCTIONS FOR SEASONING A WOK

I   To treat a new wok:

1. Wash thoroughly with hot water and detergent.
2. Rinse and dry on a heated stove.
3. Rub 2 TBS of oil on the cooking surface with a paper towel.
4. Heat wok until the cooking surface or inside turns golden brown.
5. Turn heat off. Cool. Allow to sit overnight.
6. Wipe with paper towel. The golden brown coating prevents food from sticking to the wok. A well seasoned wok will turn black in time.

II   To clean after each use:

1. Never use an abrasive cleansing agent on your wok.
2. After using, soak with water for awhile.
3. Wash the wok with warm water and mild detergent.
4. Dry thoroughly by heating on the stove burner for a few minutes.
5. If not using frequently, coat wok lightly with oil before putting it away.

Woks come in many sizes, ranging from 10 inches in diameter to the larger restaurant sizes. A 10-inch wok is ideal for a family of two. The most popular size is a 14-inch wok. It is a perfect size for cooking a whole chicken, duck, or fish.

There are round bottom woks and flat bottom woks. If you have an electric stove, you might prefer to use a flat bottom wok. Just make sure that it is heavy in weight, so it heats evenly. If you have a round bottom wok, a metal ring must be placed over the burner to hold the wok securely in place. One side of the ring is larger than the other. Place the larger side up for use on an electric range so the bottom is closer to the heat. Place the smaller side up for gas ranges, setting the wok higher above the flame.

The wok cover is usually made of aluminum and has a wooden handle. To save storage space, sometimes the handle is not attached when you buy it. The handle needs to be screwed on before use. The dome-shaped cover will encase a whole fowl during stewing, steaming, or smoking.

There are two different kinds of steam racks for woks. One is shaped like a large, round, flat plate with holes; the other is a small, round, metal rack with four legs. (See illustration on page 36). The latter rack can be used in any large pot for steaming, while the former is only used in a wok.

Bamboo steamer racks are not as practical as metal racks because they are hard to keep clean. Avoid bamboo racks when steaming seafood as the fishy smell is difficult to remove.

You can also invest in a big metal steamer for steaming—usually inexpensive because these are made from aluminum. Since the food does not actually touch the cooking surface, it will not affect the food. A metal steamer is perfect for steaming seafood, especially large fish or big crabs. The smell and grease in the food can be easily washed away in the dishwasher.

A round-edged spatula is a must when using a wok. Some chefs use the ladle with the spatula while stir-frying in large woks. Each of these utensils has a long metal handle with a wooden stub inserted to prevent the handle from getting too hot during cooking.

Strainers are used for scooping and draining deep-fried food and blanched vegetables. There are two types of strainers. One is made of brass wires with a bamboo handle. This is the traditional strainer and is hard to keep clean. To clean, soak in soapy water and use a brush to remove all food caught between the wires. The second kind of strainer is made of stainless steel. It has holes for drainage. This type is very easy to clean and can be washed in the dishwasher. Both come in various sizes. The best sizes to get are 5 inches and 10 inches in diameter. The 10 inch size is used to make Potato Bird's Nest and Golden Plate (see recipes on pages 145 and 181).

The most important piece of equipment for oriental cooking is the Chinese cleaver which comes in two types: a heavy chopper and a thin slicer. The heavier the chopper, the easier it is to use. The slicer comes in different widths. Usually the wider width (about 3½ inches) is for slicing fish and meat; the narrow blade (about 2½ to 2¾ inches) is for cutting vegetables. Cleavers come in carbon steel or stainless steel. Carbon steel blades will rust if not dried properly but are easy to sharpen. Stainless steel blades do not rust, but they are harder to sharpen.

The Chinese cleaver is very versatile. You can use it as a meat tenderizer by pounding meat with the back of the blade. The flat of the cleaver blade can easily loosen garlic skin with a whack. It can also be used to smash ginger and scallions to release their flavor.

The proper way to hold a cleaver is to hold the handle with 3 fingers and stabilize the blade with the thumb and index finger on either side of the blade. This allows you to bear down with your whole arm while cutting instead of using only your fingers and wrist.

Hold the food with your fingers tucked under, pressing it with your fingertips. Cut carefully with the flat of the blade held against the knuckles, using them as a guide. Lift the cleaver only a little to ensure efficient and safe cutting. With practice, you will be able to cut, slice, chop, and mince like an expert.

To keep cleavers in perfect condition, use a good sharpening steel and a good sharpening stone. To sharpen the cleaver or knife, hold the steel vertically in one hand with the point of the steel firmly placed on a cutting board. Place the cleaver at the top of the steel with the cleaver handle close to the sharpening steel. Bring the blade down with medium pressure at a 20° angle, pulling the handle towards you as you go down the steel (see illustrations below). Alternate from left to right to sharpen both sides of the blade. Four or five strokes on the steel should restore the edge.

HOW TO USE A SHARPENING STEEL

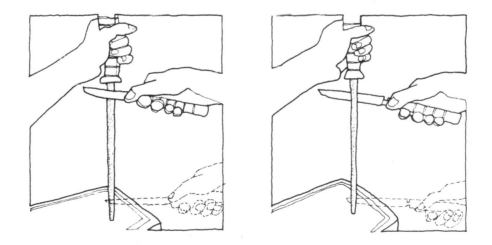

Sharpening stones come in many sizes. The larger the stone, the easier it is to use. Place the blade over the stone and rub it with medium pressure to smooth all rough edges. Add a few drops of oil.

Never wash cleavers or knives in the dishwasher. Edges are dulled and blades damaged by contact with other objects. Always wash this equipment by hand with soap and warm water. Dry separately by holding the sharp edge away from your hand. Use a dry cloth to wipe blades from the heel to the tip.

Most Chinese chefs like to use large, round, wooden cutting boards that work best with cleavers. Only in recent years has wood been replaced with man-made materials, which can be sterilized in dishwashers. Wood is harder to keep clean. The best way to clean a wooden board is to bleach it overnight.

A last, but not least, item of equipment to have is an electric rice cooker. It works like a toaster as everything is automatic. Measure rice and water according to instructions. Rice steams to perfection and stays warm until ready to serve. A rice cooker can also be used for reheating leftovers and for steaming bread and vegetables. A good size to buy is one that cooks four to six cups of rice. Brands such as Tatung, Hitachi, and National are all excellent and will last through many years of daily usage.

METHODS OF COOKING

Stir-frying is the most common method used in Chinese cooking. I can still remember, as a child in school, watching a lady cook lunch on a little wood burning stove on the veranda across from my classroom. It smelled so good. In no time, she had cooked several dishes in her wok on a little brazier. Stir-frying requires less cooking time than other methods and also conserves expensive fuel. No wonder stir-frying has become so popular for people with a limited amount of time to spend in the kitchen.

The wok, a large skillet, or a frying pan, are most appropriate for stir-frying. Read the recipe in advance to see which ingredients are needed and preparations required. Dried ingredients, like black mushrooms and black fungus, need to be soaked first to soften. Seafood and meat need to be washed, cut, and marinated at room temperature. Vegetables need to be washed, drained, and cut. Seasoning sauces and thickening sauces, made with cornstarch, need to be mixed. Line up all ingredients next to the range in the order they will be used in cooking. Heat the wok or frying pan before adding vegetable oil. This will prevent food from sticking. Cook the ingredients separately. For example, cook seafood first, remove and drain, add more oil, and then cook the vegetables. When vegetables are tender-crisp, add seafood and stir together. Serve stir-fried dishes immediately. Timing is very critical. Do not overcook.

Braising is a method used often for home cooking. First brown the food in oil, then cook in a small amount of liquid or sauce over low heat for a period of time. Braising takes about 15 to 30 minutes. Use the wok or a heavy metal pot, such as a dutch oven, for best results. The food can be easily reheated or eaten cold and still taste very good.

Deep-frying is more popular for restaurant cooking because most people do not like to dirty their kitchens at home. The wok is an excellent utensil for deep-frying. It holds a large quantity of oil and has an ample surface area for frying. A deep pot or deep-fryer are good too. Never use a pot made of copper or lined with copper for deep-frying.

Quality and temperature of the oil are critical in deep-frying. Always use a good brand of vegetable oil and have enough oil in the pot or wok to allow the food to float freely. The more oil you use, the more constant the temperature will be, and the faster the food will cook with a less greasy taste. Used oil can be cooled, strained, and stored in jars in the refrigerator for future use. Store oil used to fry seafood in one jar and oil used to fry meat and vegetables in a second jar. Oil may be reused a few times until it becomes too dark in color or foams too much while cooking. Deep-frying a few potato slices will lighten the color.

To test the temperature of oil, drop a small piece of bread or wonton wrapper into the oil. The oil should foam around the test food. Many Chinese use the chopsticks test by putting a pair of dry, wooden chopsticks in the oil to see if the oil foams around them or not. Hot oil will foam. The oil should not be too hot or smoking. This burns the food outside but does not cook the food inside. If the oil is too cool, the food will take too long to cook, and the results will be greasy. Cook a few pieces of food at a time. Do not crowd the pan. This lowers the temperature of the oil. After frying, drain the food on double layers of paper towels which have been placed on top of newspaper and brown paper bags.

If you are deep-frying a large quantity of food, fry in two stages. Lightly fry until just pale golden brown, remove and drain well. You may freeze or refrigerate the food at this point. When ready to serve, deep-fry quickly again in hot oil to heat through and to crisp. This method is used in many restaurants. It is called "deep-fry twice."

Steaming is used instead of baking in China. For centuries, the Chinese did not have ovens in their kitchens. Bread in China is always steamed. Steaming is a healthy way of preparing food because it uses very little or no oil. Food always tastes so juicy and tender cooked this way, and more nutrients are retained.

There are several ways to steam food. The easiest is to steam in a large metal steamer or on a steam rack or steam plate in the wok. Fill the wok with enough water to come within an inch of the top of the rack; bring to a boil. Place food on a heat-proof serving dish and put on the rack. Timing is critical for seafood and vegetables but not for meat and bread. For example, when steaming fish, a good rule is 8 minutes per pound. However for bread, you may steam and re-steam. It will not harm the bread nor overcook it.

A good way to improvise a steamer is to use the largest pot you have. Set one or two heat-proof bowls (any china bowl will do) right side up in the pot (see illustration below).

HOW TO IMPROVISE FOR STEAMING

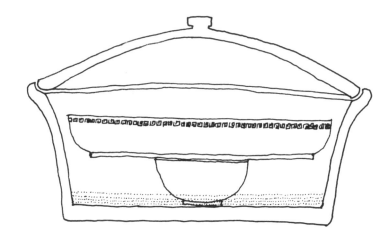

An important tip for successful steaming is to boil the water just before putting the food in the steamer. This is like pre-heating the oven. Boil a few inches of water. Place the food in a heat-proof dish over the bowl. Make sure there is enough space around the edge of the dish to allow the steam to rise and circulate freely. Be careful when removing the cover of the pot. It can be extremely hot. Set it quickly in the sink, since it may be dripping with collected vapor. Wear rubber gloves to protect your hands from the heat and steam and to remove the dish carefully. Serve in the cooking dish.

Baking is seldom done in China. In fact, baking has only existed for the last few hundred years. The Cantonese learned how to bake from Westerners. When I went back to Shanghai, China in 1979, none of my relatives had ovens in their kitchens. I don't believe many of them do even today.

For best results when baking Chinese dishes, marinate the food well in advance. Flavor is enhanced if food is marinated at room temperature for half an hour to an hour. Longer marinating requires refrigeration, especially for seafood. Overbaking dries the food. Baste often to enhance the flavor. Always preheat the oven before using, and remove the food promptly when done.

In Chinese cooking, a combination of cooking methods is often used. For instance, vegetables may be parboiled, then stir-fried. Parboiling is a method used to cook food quickly in a large pot with 6 to 8 cups of boiling water. This process seals in vitamins and tenderizes ingredients. Vegetables cooked this way become more intense in color. It is a good method to use when cooking several ingredients. You can use the same pot of water to parboil all the ingredients in a recipe. A perfect example is the Sauteed Vegetable

Medley dish on page 180. Tofu should always be parboiled or sealed in oil before stir-frying. This enhances the flavor and prevents it from falling apart while stir-frying.

Sealing in oil is a method called "Yo-Pao" and is used by many Chinese chefs. It tenderizes and seals in the flavor of food. It is different from deep-frying in that the food is cooked quickly in oil and is removed as soon as the color changes. Often it takes only a few seconds to a minute. The oil is not as hot as for deep-frying. For seafood and tofu, 300°F is hot enough. The oil can be reused for stir-frying.

Smoking is frequently used in dishes from Hunan and Szechuan provinces. It flavors rather than actually cooks the food. However, fish will cook while being smoked (see recipe on page 121). The simplest way to smoke fish is to place it on the top rack of an oven and place a tray of tea leaves and brown sugar on the bottom rack. If your oven does not have a vent, then you may prefer to smoke outdoors in a domed smoker. A disposable foil tray with tea leaves and brown sugar can be placed directly above the charcoal and below the fish on the rack.

There are many other methods of cooking used in China. The most common ones are mentioned in this cookbook. For specific instructions, read the beginning of each chapter as well as the recipes.

HOW TO REHEAT

Most Chinese dishes do not reheat well. This is especially true for seafood and vegetables because cooking time is so critical in order to avoid overcooking. The best way to reheat is in a microwave oven. The flavor and texture of the food are least altered by this method.

To reheat in a microwave, use a microwave safe dish, (glassware, china, or pottery without metal trim); dishwasher safe, rigid plastic containers; cooking bags; or paper products. Use dishes that are best suited for microwave cooking. Round dishes are better than square ones because cooking is more even. Use lids and covers to keep heat and steam in. Vented plastic wrap is equally effective in retaining heat and moisture. Use waxed paper and paper towels for food that needs less moisture and heat retention to cook. This also reduces spattering when cooking.

There are many factors that affect cooking time when using the microwave. The more food that is cooked at one time, the longer it will take to cook or reheat. Larger and bulkier pieces of food will take longer than smaller, thinner pieces. Cut food into smaller pieces for more even heating. The density and temperature of the food will also affect cooking time.

A microwave reheats food quickly but not always evenly. Usually it takes 4 to 5 minutes to reheat a dish. Half way through heating, turn and stir the food to cook it all the way through. Move the heated portions from the edge to the center and the cooler center portions to the edge where they can cook faster. Stirring also prevents overcooking at the edges. Check for doneness by feeling the center of the bottom of the dish itself with your fingers. If it is hot, the food is heated through. If it is not hot, the food is still cool. Always allow the reheated food to stand a few minutes before serving, as cooking continues after food comes out of a microwave oven. It is advisable to undercook food slightly, allowing cooking to finish during the standing time.

Deep-fried foods do not microwave well. The best way to reheat deep-fried foods is to set them on a rack and reheat them 10 to 15 minutes in a preheated oven (about 300°F to 375°F). Half-way through warming, turn food for even browning. Another method of reheating is to deep-fry a second time. This method is most commonly used in restaurants. If you have only a few pieces to reheat, use a tabletop oven broiler. Watch closely so food does not burn.

HOW TO MEASURE

Students often ask me if I actually measure all my ingredients and follow recipes exactly. I always answer them with this comment: "If you want good results each time you cook, then follow each recipe closely and measure accurately, especially the first few times." Cooking is an art and a science. An expert chef samples food as he or she cooks. It is like being an artist who knows all the art principles but chooses to create his own. This is the same with cooking. An experienced cook knows all the theories behind preparing each dish so he or she may not need a recipe. But for a beginner, it is important to learn how to cook the Chinese way first. When the techniques are perfected, then one does not need to follow directions exactly.

Being trained as a Home Economist, I've been taught that if you know how to read and follow directions you'll know how to cook. This is the scientific approach to cooking, and it works. When you try the recipes in this book for the first time, follow the steps as written and measure each ingredient precisely. Your dinner will surely turn out to be a great success.

To measure, use a standard set of ¼, ½, 1 teaspoon, ½, and 1 tablespoon measuring spoons for both dry and liquid ingredients. Always level off with the straight edge of a knife.

For stock or other liquid ingredients, use a 1 or 2 cup liquid measuring cup. The glass ones are excellent for the microwave and easy to read. Always read the line on the measuring cup at eye level when checking the volume of liquid in a cup.

For dry ingredients, such as flour, use a set of graduated metal measuring cups, consisting of ⅛, ¼, ⅓, ½ and 1 cup measures. Again, level off with the straight edge of a knife.

Recipes in this cookbook use abbreviated letters in the measurements. They are as follows:

tsp	=	teaspoon
TBS	=	tablespoon
lb	=	pound
oz	=	ounce

Many people are now on low sodium diets. If necessary, you may use less salt than the recipe calls for or use low-sodium salt instead of regular salt. You may also dilute soy sauce with water or use light soy sauce in order to cut down on the amount of sodium. In sweet and sour dishes, some people prefer a sweeter sauce and may add more sugar or may use brown sugar instead. Always taste every dish before serving.

METHODS OF CUTTING

Cutting is extremely important in Chinese cooking, especially when stir-frying. Cutting improves flavor because more area is exposed to seasoning agents. More nutrients are retained because less time is required to cook the food.

There are three main factors in determining how to cut a given ingredient. The first factor is the nature of the ingredient, how tough or tender it is. The tougher the ingredient, the smaller you should cut it, because this reduces cooking time. Tender foods need not be cut as small since these cook faster.

The second factor is how the ingredient is to be cooked, which method of cooking is being used. For braising or deep-frying, the ingredient is usually cut into 1" or 2" pieces. For stir-frying, it is often cut smaller.

The third factor is what sizes and shapes of food are being combined. For example, in a recipe calling for green peas, most likely all ingredients are diced. Ingredients cooked with bean sprouts are usually shredded. A good principle to remember for stir-frying is that all ingredients are usually cut into similar sizes and shapes so as to cook evenly and to achieve visual harmony and uniformity.

The most common cutting methods are slicing, shredding, dicing, and roll cutting (see illustration on page 46). Slicing can be straight or diagonal. For tender ingredients, such as mushrooms and tofu, always slice straight, which means holding the cleaver perpendicular to the food. Diagonal slicing is for tougher ingredients, such as carrots and broccoli stems. Hold the cleaver at a 45° angle to the food and slice. This is done to expose more area for faster cooking. When a recipe calls for slicing, the pieces are usually 1½"-2" long, 1" wide and ⅛"- ¼" thick.

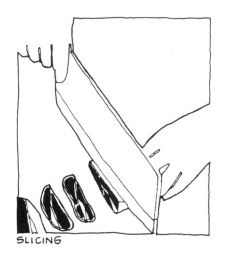

SLICING

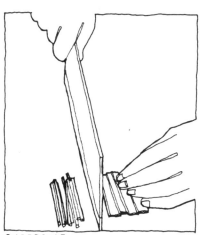

SHREDDING

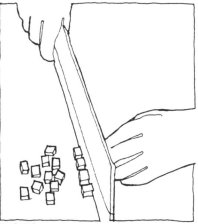

DICING

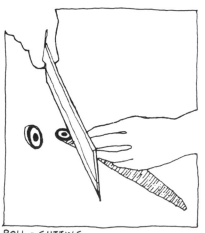

ROLL-CUTTING

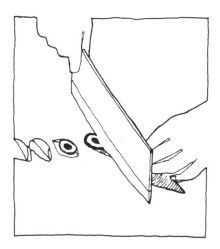

Shredded ingredients should resemble matchsticks and measure 2" long, ½" wide and ⅛" thick. For salads and decorations, vegetables such as green onions may be shredded even thinner.

To dice, you must first cut the ingredients into strips, then crosswise into cubes. Dicing comes in several sizes. For deep-frying and slow cooking, cut ½" to 2" dice. For stir-frying, cut ⅛" to ½" dice.

Roll cutting is used for cylindrical vegetables such as carrots, turnips, and daikon. To roll cut, hold your cleaver at a 45° angle, make a diagonal slice straight down, then roll the ingredient a quarter turn and slice again. This size and shape are often used for stewed and braised dishes.

If you are serving several stir-fried dishes at a time, make sure each is different in size and shape. Otherwise, all the food will look and seem to taste alike.

Years ago, before the invention of the food processor, Chinese cooks used their cleavers to mince meat and seafood. I can still remember the cook at home, banging away with two cleavers, one in each hand, mincing meat or shrimp. Today, mincing with a cleaver is mainly for garlic and ginger. For best results, slice the garlic paper thin first, then shred and mince. Hold the tip of the cleaver down with one hand while lifting the handle slightly with the other hand, moving back and forth until the garlic is finely minced.

Scoring is used on fish, squid, and meat. Scoring means making parallel cuts about ¼" to ½" deep, to speed cooking and improve flavor. This is especially true when cooking a whole fish. The flesh close to the fish head is always thicker than the tail and needs deeper scoring. Proper scoring helps the entire fish cook evenly.

HELPFUL HINTS

✧ Read the book, especially the beginning of each chapter. This will help you to understand the techniques better.

✧ Start with a simple recipe. All recipes with difficulty level 1 are easy to follow. When you feel confident with these, try difficulty level 2 and finally level 3.

✧ Read the entire recipe and gather all ingredients before beginning to cook.

✧ Allow extra time to cook when trying a recipe for the first time. Also, it is easier to try one new dish at a time.

✧ Accent or Monosodium Glutimate (MSG) is not used in this cookbook. Be sure to cook with a good stock to improve flavor (see soup on page 81).

✧ Use lemon, lime, or toothpaste to wash your hands after cooking with seafood. This will remove all fishy odors.

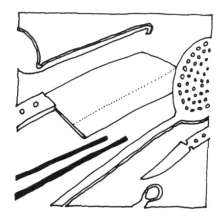

興共病時服藥 不如今補養生

"It is better to eat nutritious food and maintain good health,
than take medicine when sick."

HOW TO STAY HEALTHY
AND SLIM

INTRODUCTION

THE BASIC CHINESE DIET

RECOMMENDATIONS FOR MAINTAINING
A HEALTHY BODY

HOW TO PLAN A HEALTHY MENU

THE CHINESE WAY OF MENU PLANNING

Chinese menu planning is very different from American menu planning. In China, there is no single main dish. Every dish is just as important as the others. Most Westerners plan a dinner by deciding which meat or seafood to serve; then the side dishes such as potatoes, vegetables, and salads are selected to go with the main course. This is not so with Chinese menu planning.

An average Chinese meal used to be one soup and four dishes, the four dishes being as follows: seafood, meat often cooked with vegetables, tofu or eggs, and vegetables. Today, less help is available in the kitchen, and more people are working outside their homes. Most meals now consist of soup or salad and two dishes. This is what I serve my family of four. The two dishes are a protein dish and a vegetable dish, served with steamed rice, and fresh fruit as dessert.

THE FOUR ELEMENTS IN MENU PLANNING

1. Color

2. Aroma

3. Flavor

4. Nutritional balance

We eat not only with our mouths but also with our eyes, nose, tongue, and touch. A beautiful presentation of color will entice any diner. To achieve this, always try to visualize the menu in terms of color. For instance, if you are serving Shrimp with Lobster Sauce, it is a good idea to serve it with a green vegetable, such as snow peas or asparagus, and a colorful salad.

One of my students went to a dinner party. She told the class that she was served white turkey breast, mashed potatoes, and cauliflower. It was quite a shock to see all this white colored food set before her. But once she started to eat, she said the dinner turned out to be quite delicious.

Fragrant aroma is achieved by using different seasonings and spices. Sweet and sour sauce always smells mouthwatering. Fermented black beans with garlic is another favorite of my family. Try to avoid using two powerful seasonings in one meal. It is best to serve one mild dish with one that is pungent in aroma.

To illustrate how important the aroma is, one of my students shared her secret with the class. When she was pregnant, she did not feel like cooking one day. So, just before her husband came home, she put two TV dinners in the oven and browned a clove of garlic with butter on the stove. When her husband arrived home, he said, "Honey, dinner smells wonderful!"

Once the food looks appetizing and smells wonderful, you expect it to taste good. The texture and flavor of any dish depend upon the cooking method and seasoning. It is important to use different methods of cooking in a meal. For example, try to visualize a meal where everything is deep-fried. The meal becomes too crunchy and greasy. A better menu has only one dish deep-fried, while another is steamed, and the third stir-fried or braised.

For nutritional balance, I cannot emphasize enough the importance of the Basic Four in meal planning. An adult only needs two servings of dairy products, two servings of protein, four servings of vegetables and fruit, and four servings of grain per day.

THE BASIC FOUR FOR ADULTS			
2 Servings	2 Servings	4 Servings	4 Servings
Dairy Products	Protein	Vegetables & Fruits	Grain
Tofu	Fish	Snow Peas	Rice
Milk	Shrimp	Bok Choy	Bread
Cheese	Chicken	Salads	Noodles
	Eggs	Apples	Pancakes
	Meat	Oranges	Cereal

If you have cereal with milk for breakfast and tofu for lunch, you do not need to eat a dairy product at the evening meal. Adults who eat two servings of dairy products will only need 4 ounces of cooked seafood or meat per day. However, children, teenagers, pregnant women, and nursing mothers need four servings of dairy products and protein daily.

HELPFUL CHECKLIST IN MENU PLANNING

✧ Do I have a variety of colors in my menu?

✧ Am I using different seasonings in each dish?

✧ Am I using different cooking methods?

✧ Do I have enough servings from each Basic Four Group to meet my daily nutritional needs?

✧ Am I repeating a particular food in several dishes?

EXAMPLE OF A MENU EVALUATION					
Menu #1	Color	Seasoning	Method of Cooking	Basic 4	Ingredients
Egg Flower Soup	Yellow	Light	Egg & Chicken Boiled	Protein	Stock
Fish Fillets w/ Oyster Sauce	White & Brown	Rich Oyster Sauce	Stir-Fried	Protein & Vegetable	Fish, Tomatoes & Carrots
Baked Chinese Cabbage w/Crab Sauce	Green, White & Red	Mild Crab Sauce	Stir-Fried and Baked	Vegetable & Protein	Chinese Cabbage & Crab
Rice	White	Bland	Steamed	Grain	Rice
Orange Slices	Orange	Sweet & Sour	Cold	Fruit	Orange

20 SUGGESTED MENUS

The following are just a few examples of how to combine the recipes in this cookbook. Now that you know the basic theory in Chinese menu planning, you may change or add dishes to these menus as you please. I have included 10 menu suggestions for 4 to 6 persons and another 10 menus for 6 to 8 persons. The menus are arranged from easy dinners to more elaborate ones.

If you are cooking for only two people and want a quick and easy menu, choose a recipe that includes vegetables and protein. Examples of these dishes are Stir-fried Shrimp with Cashews or Butterfly Shrimp with Snow Peas. Serve these with steamed rice and fruit for dessert. Or, you may cut the recipes in the first 10 menus in half. If you do not mind eating the same food the next day, just prepare the entire menu but serve only half the amount in each dish. This way you have cooked enough for a second meal.

Whenever an unexpected guest arrives at the last minute, the best solution is to add one more dish. My mother often served scrambled eggs with diced tomato or opened a can of braised bamboo shoots or fried fish.

Most Chinese stir-fried recipes do not double well because there are too many ingredients in the wok which changes the cooking time. However, you can make the recipe one and half times, or cook the recipe twice and mix them together to serve.

If you like simple menus, the easiest way is to choose a fish or seafood dish and serve it with a basic stir-fried vegetable or salad. For my family, I usually spend an hour preparing my dinners. I save the more elaborate dishes, such as Sauteed Vegetable Medley and Squirrel Fish with Sweet and Sour Sauce, for special occasions.

Once I asked my mother whether it bothered her to spend so much time cooking every day. Her answer was, " To live is to enjoy food. What else is there in life but to cook and eat?"

MENU #1

Egg Flower Soup (Pg. 83)

Fish Fillet with Oyster Sauce (Pg. 123)

Baked Chinese Cabbage with Crab Sauce (Pg. 177)

Steamed Rice (Pg. 31)

Orange Slices

✧   ✧   ✧

MENU #2

Celery and Carrot Salad (Pg. 99)

Shrimp with Green Peas (Pg. 134)

Pan-fried Tofu, Beijing Style (Pg. 157)

Steamed Rice (Pg. 31)

Strawberries with Powdered Sugar

✧   ✧   ✧

MENU #3

Steamed Egg Soup (Pg. 91)

Smoked and Baked Fish Steaks (Pg. 121)

Chinese String Beans with Bean Thread (Pg. 178)

Steamed Rice (Pg. 31)

Asian Pears

✧   ✧   ✧

MENU #4

Crispy Salad with Puffed Rice Sticks (Pg. 110)

Stir-fried Shrimp with Cashews (Pg. 137)

Steamed Rice (Pg. 31)

Assorted Fresh Fruit in Season

MENU #5

Three Flavor Soup (Pg. 84)

Steamed Flounder, Cantonese Style (Pg. 128)

Green Beans with Water Chestnuts (Pg. 172)

Steamed Rice (Pg. 31)

Red and Green Grapes

✧   ✧   ✧

MENU #6

Carrot, Cucumber and Daikon Salad (Pg. 97)

Shrimp with Lobster Sauce (Pg. 136)

Stir-fried Asparagus (Pg. 168)

Steamed Rice (Pg. 31)

Cantaloupe and Honeydew Cubes

✧   ✧   ✧

MENU #7

Crab and Spinach Soup (Pg. 88)

Butterfly Shrimp with Snow Peas and Straw Mushrooms (Pg. 139)

Bok Choy with Cream Sauce (Pg. 174)

Steamed Rice (Pg. 31)

Mango Wedges with Seedless Grapes (Pg. 191)

✧   ✧   ✧

MENU #8

Cucumber and Tomato Salad (Pg. 98)

Deep-fried Flounder (Pg. 117)

Braised Tofu with Ham (Pg. 161)

Steamed Rice (Pg. 31)

Fresh Plums and Peaches

✧　　✧　　✧

MENU #9

Watercress and Water Chestnut Salad (Pg. 108)

Fish Fillets with Tomato Sauce (Pg. 118)

Baked Savory Tofu with Mixed Vegetables (Pg. 162)

Steamed Rice (Pg. 31)

Papaya Halves

✧　　✧　　✧

MENU #10

Watercress and Fish Fillet Soup (Pg. 85)

Sweet and Sour Shrimp (Pg. 135)

Stir-fried Napa Cabbage (Pg. 168)

Steamed Rice (Pg. 31)

Red Delicious Apples

✧　　✧　　✧

MENU #11

Pan-fried Shrimp Dumplings (Pg. 76)

Agar Agar Salad with Spicy Dressing (Pg. 105)

Steamed Fish Steaks with Peppers (Pg. 120)

Sauteed Tofu, Family Style (Pg. 158)

Steamed Rice (Pg. 31)

Watermelon Shell Filled with Fruit (Pg. 194)

✧　　✧　　✧

✧   ✧   ✧

MENU #12

Crispy Fish on Toast (Pg. 73)

Clams with Golden Mushrooms Soup (Pg. 86)

Steamed Flower-shaped Prawns with Chinese Green Cabbage (Pg. 142)

Tofu with Oyster Sauce (Pg. 153)

Steamed Rice (Pg. 31)

Almond Float (Pg. 189)

✧   ✧   ✧

MENU #13

Shrimp Balls (Pg. 68)

Bean Sprouts Salad with Ham Garnish (Pg. 103)

Steamed Trout with Ginger Sauce (Pg. 116)

Hunan Asparagus with Black Bean Sauce (Pg. 182)

Steamed Rice (Pg. 31)

Spun Apples (Pg. 196)

✧   ✧   ✧

MENU #14

Egg Rolls with Shrimp (Pg. 74)

Tomato with Sweet Corn Soup (Pg. 93)

Steamed Fish with Fermented Black Beans (Pg. 124)

Baked Savory Tofu with Spinach (Pg. 156)

Steamed Rice (Pg. 31)

Sesame Seed Cookies and Fresh Fruit (Pg. 193)

✧   ✧   ✧

✧   ✧   ✧

MENU #15

Green Onion Pancakes (Pg. 67)

Hot and Sour Soup (Pg. 94)

Crispy Shrimp with Garlic (Pg. 133)

Braised Mushrooms with Spinach (Pg. 176)

Steamed Rice (Pg. 31)

Steamed Pears with Honey (Pg. 187)

✧   ✧   ✧

MENU #16

Fried Shrimp Wonton (Pg. 72)

Fresh Asparagus Salad (Pg. 101)

Fish Fillets with Fermented Black Beans (Pg. 122)

Snow Peas with Mushrooms and Bamboo Shoots (Pg. 171)

Steamed Rice (Pg. 31)

Almond Cookies and Fresh Fruit (Pg. 192)

✧   ✧   ✧

MENU #17

Braised Mushrooms (Pg. 71)

Crab Meat and Cucumber Salad (Pg. 104)

Seafood in a Potato Bird's Nest (Pg. 144 & 145)

Broccoli with Oyster Sauce (Pg. 173)

Steamed Rice (Pg. 31)

Steamed Cake (Pg. 195)

✧   ✧   ✧

✧ ✧ ✧

MENU #18

Steamed Shrimp Shao Mai (Pg. 70)

Spinach Velvet Soup (Pg. 90)

Crispy Fish Slices with Sweet and Sour Sauce (Pg. 119)

Sauteed Vegetable Medley on the Golden Plate (Pg. 180 & 181)

Steamed Rice (Pg. 31)

Three Exotic Fruits on Crushed Ice (Pg. 186)

✧ ✧ ✧

MENU #19

Shrimp Toast (Pg. 66)

Sizzling Rice Soup (Pg. 92)

Stir-fried Squid, Szechuan Style (Pg. 146)

Mushrooms with Tofu (Pg. 155)

Steamed Rice (Pg. 31)

Pineapple Boats with Cherries (Pg. 191)

✧ ✧ ✧

MENU #20

Miniature Shrimp Pears (Pg. 77)

Baked Seafood in Swan-shaped Foil Packets (Pg. 140)

Stir-fried Vegetables with Baby Corn (Pg. 175)

Ma-Po's Tofu with Hot Sauce (Pg. 160)

Steamed Rice (Pg. 31)

Butterfly Cookies and Fresh Fruit (Pg. 190)

✧ ✧ ✧

藥補不如食補行

"Eating the right food is better
than taking the right medicine."

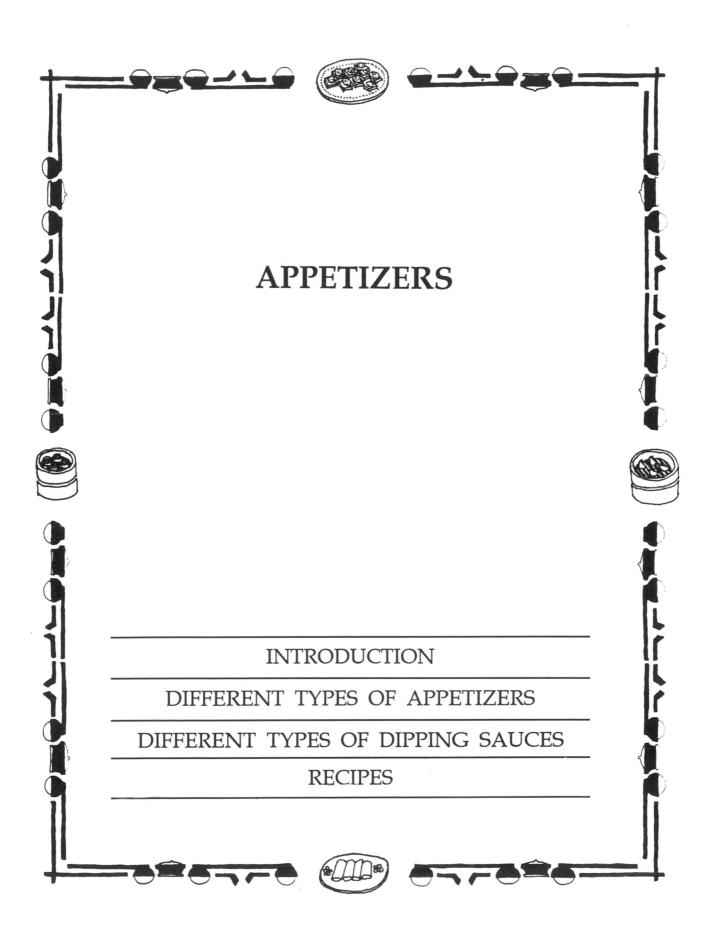

APPETIZERS

APPETIZERS

INTRODUCTION

When I lived in Hong Kong, my father once ordered a 100 course banquet fit for an Emperor. It was a feast to be remembered. We sat around the largest table we could find, which was a ping pong table. All our relatives came and joined us that evening. Before we even sat down for dinner, about 20 assorted appetizers had already been placed on the table. There were nuts, dried fruits, seeds, candies, and a scrumptious array of cold cuts, smoked seafood, and pickled vegetables.

In China, it is common to start a banquet with a beautiful arrangement of cold platters. They are placed on the table before the guests are seated and serve as centerpieces. Sometimes the appetizers are ornately arranged into a phoenix or dragon design. They may be as elaborate as the chef chooses. The purpose of cold platters is to whet the diners' appetites and satisfy hunger until the hot food is served.

Chinese seldom drink alcoholic beverages before dinner. Wines and liquors are served when everyone is seated at the table with the cold platter. It is not a Chinese custom to serve hot hors d'oeuvres with cocktails; therefore, most of the hot dishes in this chapter would be served as part of a main course.

When planning a formal dinner party, if you would like to serve two kinds of hors d'oeuvres, serve one cold and one hot appetizer. The cold appetizer can be made ahead and placed on the coffee table for the guests to serve themselves. The hot appetizer can be cooked or reheated after all the guests have arrived.

DIFFERENT TYPES OF APPETIZERS

Basically, there are only two main categories of appetizers—cold appetizers and hot hors d'oeuvres. A cold appetizer is more popular because it may be prepared days ahead. A typical cold platter consists of thin slices of steamed chicken, braised beef, roast pork, abalone, and ham. Smoked fish, shrimp with tomato sauce, and sweet and sour cabbage are often included.

Hot hors d'oeuvres are served mainly as snacks between meals or as part of dinner. In the Southern part of China, Dim Sum dishes, such as Steamed Dumplings and Egg Rolls, are served in the Tea Houses where people go after shopping or the movies.

Besides the above appetizers, Chinese often serve nuts or chips for guests to nibble. Prawn crackers or shrimp chips are one of my favorite party appetizers. They are made from prawns, starch, salt, and sugar and can be purchased in Chinese grocery stores.

Cooked chips are sold in plastic bags like potato chips. Uncooked chips are packaged in boxes. To prepare uncooked chips, simply deep-fry in hot oil. These will keep in an airtight container until ready to serve. Shrimp chips are pale pink in color or dyed in different colors, such as yellow, green, or white. The plain chips are crispier but not as festive. Chefs often use them as a garnish for deep-fried dishes, such as Crispy Duck or Garlic Shrimp.

Another popular appetizer is dried fruit. Chinese preserve many kinds of fruits, such as plums or lychees. These are coated with a variety of seasonings and spices. Some are sweet, others sour, and some are spicy hot. These dried fruits are high in fiber and low in calories. They will keep in the cupboard for several months to enjoy as between meal snacks.

Watermelon and pumpkin seeds are often served with dried fruits. These come in many flavors and are nutritious. Seeds are high in protein and contain no cholesterol. Since seeds symbolize fertility, they are frequently served at wedding banquets and New Year's celebrations.

DIFFERENT TYPES OF DIPPING SAUCES

Fried foods in China are dipped in Flavored Pepper Salt, which is salt stir-fried with Szechuan peppercorn (see recipe on page 64). Another popular dip is soy sauce with vinegar. Diners usually mix their own sauces. Some people like a lot of vinegar with their soy sauce, and some like less. Many Cantonese restaurants serve ketchup with fried foods. The word ketchup comes from the Chinese word "Koi Tsiap" according to the American Heritage Dictionary of the English Language. Many sweet and sour sauces use ketchup to give the red color that symbolizes happiness in China.

Most dipping sauces are sold in glass jars in Oriental markets. They can be used as is or mixed with other ingredients to enhance the flavor. For instance, you can pour the plum sauce right out of the bottle to serve with the hors d'oeuvres or mix it with crushed pineapple or applesauce.

For those who enjoy spicy food, there is a great variety of hot chili and mustard sauces available. Often restaurants serve a hot chili oil that comes in a bottle and looks red in color. You can use it with most appetizers.

Keep opened, bottled sauces in the refrigerator if you are not planning to use them right away. Hot chili oil and soy sauce need no refrigeration. They will keep for a long time at room temperature.

花椒塩

FLAVORED PEPPER SALT

This salt and pepper mixture is very fragrant.   It can be made ahead and kept in a glass jar to be served with any fried food.

Makes 3 TBS of pepper salt   **Difficulty level 1**

---

1   TBS Szechuan peppercorns   2   TBS salt

1. In dry wok, cook peppercorns and salt about 1 minute over low heat. When the salt is browned and smells good, remove from heat and cool.

2. In a mortar or coffee bean grinder, grind finely. Sift through a fine sieve.

甜酸醬

SWEET AND SOUR SAUCE

There are many variations of sweet and sour sauces. You may adjust the amount of sugar and vinegar to suit your own taste.

Makes 1 1/2 cups sauce   **Difficulty level 1**

1	TBS salad oil	1/4	cup packed brown sugar
1	clove garlic, minced	2	TBS ketchup
1/2	cup cold water	1/2	TBS soy sauce
1/3	cup cider vinegar	1	TBS cornstarch mixed
1	can (8 oz) crushed pineapple and juice		with 1 TBS water

1. Heat oil in a small pan over medium heat. Add minced garlic and stir for a few seconds until fragrant.

2. Add next 6 ingredients and bring to a boil. Add cornstarch mixture and stir until thickened.

CHINESE PLUM SAUCE

You may use the plum sauce as is or follow the recipe below for a different flavor.

Makes 3/4 cup sauce   Difficulty level 1

1	dried red pepper (optional)
1/2	cup Chinese plum sauce
1/4	cup canned crushed pineapple*

1. Cut dried red peppers into ¼" pieces. Remove tip and seeds.

2. Blend all ingredients together and serve in a small bowl.

* Canned applesauce may be substituted for crushed pineapple.

HOT MUSTARD SAUCE

Mix dry mustard with hot water instead of cold water if you like it really hot. Let the sauce breathe at room temperature before serving to avoid harshness.

Makes 3 TBS sauce   Difficulty level 1

2	TBS dry mustard
2	TBS cold water
1/4	tsp sesame oil

1. Put mustard in a bowl. Gradually add water to mustard, stirring in a little at a time until smooth.

2. Add sesame oil and mix well. Let stand at room temperature for ½ hour before serving.

蝦仔吐司

SHRIMP TOAST

The first time I had this dish was at a banquet in China. Shrimp toast makes a perfect appetizer because it can be deep-fried and kept frozen until ready to use. To reheat, place on a cookie sheet in 350° F oven for 10-15 minutes. Drain on paper towels.

Makes 40 triangles   **Difficulty level 1**

5	water chestnuts	1	tsp dry sherry
2	strips bacon	10	slices white bread
1	lb raw shrimp, shelled & deveined		parsley leaves for garnish
1	egg white	3	cups salad oil
1	tsp salt		

1. In food processor with knife blade or manually with cleaver, chop water chestnuts into small pieces. Add bacon and shrimp; mix until finely chopped. Add egg white, salt, and sherry; mix well.

2. Cut crusts from bread. Cut slices diagonally into 4 triangles. Shake off crumbs.

3. Divide shrimp paste into 10 parts, one for each slice of bread. With knife, spread paste evenly into edges and corners of triangles. Gently press a parsley leaf into each.

4. Heat oil to 350° F in wok over medium-high heat. Fry 5-6 triangles at a time, shrimp side down, until edges are brown. Turn and lightly brown other side. Drain on paper towels.

GREEN ONION PANCAKES

In the northern part of China these pancakes are served as bread for breakfast and as a side dish for the fire pot. This recipe can be doubled, and the size of the pancakes can also be varied. After pan-frying, they may be kept frozen until ready to serve. Reheat in 350° F oven for 15 minutes until crispy.

Makes 10 pancakes   **Difficulty level 1**

2	cups flour
2/3	cup boiling water
1/3	cup minced green onions (2-3 onions)
2	TBS lard or vegetable shortening (room temperature)
1	tsp salt
1/2-1	cup salad oil

1. Mix flour and boiling water in a large bowl. Knead dough until smooth, about 5 minutes. Cover dough and let rest for 15 minutes.

2. Combine green onions, lard, and salt in a small bowl.

3. Divide dough into 10 pieces. On lightly floured board, with rolling pin, roll each piece into a 6" round. Spread each flattened pancake with 1 tsp onion mixture. Roll up jelly-roll fashion. Coil into snail-shaped round and tuck the end under. Flatten slightly and roll into a 4"-5" round.

4. Heat 4 TBS oil to 300° F in a heavy skillet over medium heat. Pan-fry pancake until golden brown, turning once, about 2 minutes. Add more oil as needed. Drain on paper towels.

炸 蝦 球

SHRIMP BALLS

If you are tired of serving meat balls as an appetizer, try Shrimp Balls. They are elegant and contain less fat and cholesterol.

Makes about 24 balls   **Difficulty level 2**

1	slice white bread	1	tsp salt
2	TBS chicken stock or water	1/2	tsp chopped ginger
4	water chestnuts	1	egg yolk
1	lb raw shrimp, shelled & deveined	1	egg white
1	strip bacon	3	cups salad oil

CONDIMENTS: flavored pepper salt or sweet and sour sauce

1. Cut crust from bread; tear bread into small pieces. Soak bread in chicken stock in a small bowl.

2. In food processor with knife blade or manually with cleaver, chop water chestnuts into small pieces. Add shrimp and bacon; mix until finely chopped. Add soaked bread, salt, ginger, and egg yolk; mix well.

3. Beat egg white to a froth and blend into the shrimp mixture.

4. Heat oil to 375° F in wok over medium-high heat. Squeeze a handful of shrimp mixture, making a fist and forcing the mixture up between your thumb and forefinger (Fig. 1). When it forms a ball about the size of a walnut, use a spoon to scoop off the ball, and drop it into the hot oil (Fig. 2). Dip spoon in cold water after forming each ball to prevent sticking. Fry 6 balls at a time until golden, about 2-3 minutes. Drain on paper towels. Serve hot with condiments.

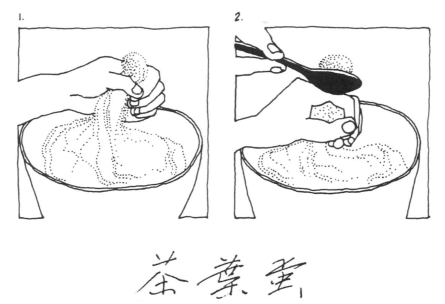

茶葉蛋

MARBLED TEA EGGS

Everywhere in China, sidewalk shops sell Tea Eggs. People buy them for breakfast and for between meal snacks. Tea eggs are also great for picnics and buffets. You can serve them hot, cold, or at room temperature. They will keep in the sauce in the refrigerator for several days.

Makes 18 servings   **Difficulty level 1**

18	small or medium-sized eggs
3	TBS black tea leaves
3	TBS soy sauce*
1	TBS star anise cloves
1/2	TBS salt

1. Put eggs in a large saucepan with cold water to cover. Hard cook eggs over medium heat, about 20 minutes.

2. Drain and rinse eggs in cold water. Crack shells by rolling eggs firmly but gently on the counter. Do not peel.

3. Put eggs in their shells and remaining ingredients in a large saucepan. Add enough water to cover. Simmer for 1 hour or more. Serve hot or cold.

* For better coloring, use 1 1/2 TBS dark soy sauce and 1 1/2 TBS regular soy sauce instead of 3 TBS regular soy sauce.

蝦仁燒賣

STEAMED SHRIMP SHAO MAI

The original recipe for Shao Mai is made with ground pork. Steamed Shao Mai means small dumpling and is served in Cantonese Tea Houses as Dim Sum. Shao Mai can be wrapped and kept frozen until ready to use.

Makes about 30 dumplings   **Difficulty level 2**

1	lb raw shrimp, shelled & deveined*	1	TBS dry sherry
4	black mushrooms, soaked & minced	1	tsp salt
1/2	cup finely chopped bamboo shoots	1/2	tsp sugar
1	TBS minced green onion	1/2	tsp sesame oil
1	TBS cornstarch	1	pkg wonton wrappers
1	TBS soy sauce	1	TBS minced carrots

CONDIMENTS: soy sauce and hot chili sauce

1. Dice shrimp. Mix shrimp with next 9 ingredients in a bowl.

2. Trim wonton wrappers into 3" rounds with cleaver. Place 1 rounded tsp of filling in center (Fig. 1). Gather sides of wrapper around filling, leaving the top open (Fig. 2). Squeeze middle gently to make sure wrapper fits firmly against filling and gives cylinder a waisted look (Fig. 3). Flatten bottom so dumpling stands upright (Fig. 4). Gently press minced carrots into top of each dumpling.

3. Place dumplings on a greased, heatproof plate or on bamboo steamers. With protective gloves, set plate on rack in wok or steamer with 1 ½"-2" of boiling water. Cover and steam over high heat for 15 minutes. Dumplings may be reheated in the steamer for 5 minutes. Serve hot with condiments.

* Ground meat such as pork, beef, chicken, or turkey may be substituted for shrimp.

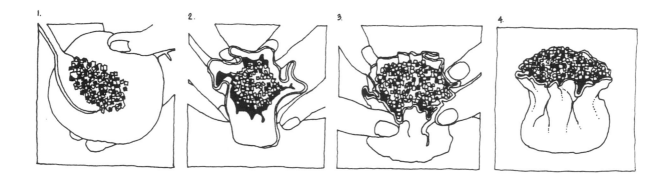

红烧冬菇

BRAISED MUSHROOMS

My mother-in-law taught me how to make this delicious and easy appetizer. Braised mushrooms are tasty hot or cold. Use as a side dish or add to stir-fried dishes. Stored in their oil, in a covered container in the refrigerator, braised mushrooms will keep for several days.

Serves 6-8   **Difficulty level 1**

1	lb fresh mushrooms
1	cup salad oil
2	TBS soy sauce
2	tsp sugar

1. Rinse and drain mushrooms. Cut a thin slice from each stem end.

2. Heat oil to 350° F in wok over medium-high heat. Fry mushrooms until caps shrink slightly, about 1-2 minutes. Add soy sauce and sugar; stir until well mixed. Reduce heat to low; cover and cook for 10 minutes, stirring once or twice for even coloring.

3. Place colander over a bowl; drain mushrooms.* Serve mushrooms hot or cold with toothpicks.

* Oil may be saved for future use in stir-frying vegetables.

炸 餛 飩

FRIED SHRIMP WONTONS

Wontons can be wrapped in advance and frozen until needed. Fried wontons can be kept warm in a 250° F oven or reheated for 5 minutes in a 450° F oven.

Makes about 4 dozen   **Difficulty level 2**

4	water chestnuts	1	tsp salt
2	green onions	1/8	tsp ground white pepper
1	lb raw shrimp, shelled & deveined	3	cups salad oil
1	tsp soy sauce	1	pkg wonton wrappers

<u>CONDIMENTS</u>: plum sauce and hot mustard sauce

1. In food processor with knife blade or manually with cleaver, mince water chestnuts with green onion. Add shrimp and chop into small pieces. Add soy sauce, salt, ground pepper, and 1 TBS oil, and mix well.

2. Place .1 tsp of shrimp mixture in center of wonton wrapper (Fig. 1). Moisten edges of wrapper with cold water. Bring corner of wrapper up over filling to opposite corner, placing points about ½" apart, forming two overlapping triangles (Fig. 2). Overlap folded edge corners and seal with water (Fig. 3). Place wontons on tray and cover with a dry towel.

3. Heat remaining oil to 350° F in wok over medium-high heat. Fry 6-8 wontons at a time until crisp and golden, about 2-3 minutes. Drain on paper towels. Serve with condiments.

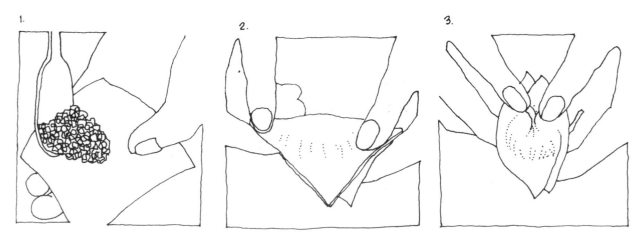

脆魚吐司

CRISPY FISH ON TOAST

Crispy fish on toast is like a mini-sandwich. It is perfect for wine tasting parties. The addition of ham adds color and flavor.

Makes 16 toasts   **Difficulty level 2**

3/4   lb fresh firm white fish (sea bass or yellow pike)
1/2   TBS cornstarch   16   thin slices ham (1 1/2" x 2")
1/2   TBS dry sherry   1/2   TBS black sesame seeds*
1/2   tsp salt   parsley leaves for garnish
8   slices white bread   3-4   cups salad oil

BATTER:
1   egg, beaten
4   TBS flour   CONDIMENTS:
2   TBS cornstarch   flavored pepper salt
2   TBS cold water   sweet and sour sauce

1. Cut fish into 16 thin slices 2" x 1 ½" x ¼". In a bowl, marinate fish with cornstarch, sherry, and salt at room temperature for 10 minutes.

2. Cut crusts from bread. Cut bread into 2" x 1 ½" pieces.

3. Mix batter ingredients in a bowl and set aside.

4. Place bread pieces on a board. Brush batter on top of bread and top with 1 slice fish. Brush again with batter. Place ham slice on fish; brush with batter. Garnish with sesame seeds and a parsley leaf.

5. Heat oil to 350° F in wok over medium-high heat. Fry a few slices of bread at a time, fish side down, until golden, about 2 minutes. Drain on paper towels. Serve hot with condiments or eat as is.

* Caviar may be used instead of black sesame seeds. Garnish after deep-frying.

蝦仁春捲

EGG ROLLS WITH SHRIMP

Egg rolls must be deep-fried immediately after wrapping, or they will become soggy. After frying, they can be frozen and reheated on a cookie rack in a 450° F oven for 15 minutes. Turn after 7 minutes for best results.

Makes about 20 egg rolls   **Difficulty level 2**

1	lb fresh bean sprouts	2	tsp salt
1	lb raw shrimp, shelled & deveined	4	cups finely shredded celery
2	TBS soy sauce	4	cups shredded cabbage
2	TBS dry sherry	1	TBS cornstarch mixed with
1	tsp sugar		2 TBS cold water
3-4	cups salad oil	1	pkg egg roll wrappers
5	fresh mushrooms, diced	1	egg, beaten

CONDIMENTS: plum sauce and hot mustard sauce

1. Wash and remove tails from bean sprouts. Dice shrimp, then mix with soy sauce, dry sherry, and sugar in a bowl.

2. Heat wok over high heat; add 2 TBS oil. When oil is hot, add mushrooms and stir until coated with oil. Add shrimp; stir until shrimp turns pink. Remove to a bowl.

3. Heat 2 TBS oil in the same wok over medium heat. Add salt, celery, and cabbage, and stir for 5 minutes. Add bean sprouts; mix well. Return shrimp mixture to wok, stirring until well combined. Stir in cornstarch mixture; cook until thickened. Transfer mixture to a colander; drain and cool.

4. Place ⅓ cup cooled filling on a wrapper. Shape filling into a cylinder about 4" long and 1" in diameter, placed diagonally across center (Fig. 1). Brush edges of wrapper with beaten egg. Lift lower triangular flap over filling and tuck point under (Fig. 2). Bring two small end flaps to top of enclosed filling forming an envelope (Fig. 3). Roll into a neat rectangular package (Fig. 4). Seal last corner with egg again. Place filled egg rolls on a tray and cover with a dry towel.

5. Heat 3-4 cups of oil to 375°F in wok. Fry 4-5 egg rolls at a time until golden brown, about 3-4 minutes. Drain on paper towels. Serve immediately with condiments.

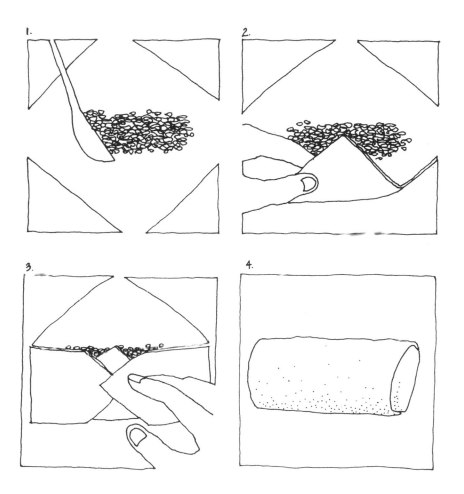

蝦 仁 鍋 貼

PAN-FRIED SHRIMP DUMPLINGS

These dumplings are also called pot-stickers because they will stick to the pan if it is not well seasoned. For best results, use a pan with a non-stick surface. Dumplings can be wrapped ahead and kept frozen until ready to pan-fry; no need to defrost. In Beijing, dumplings are served as the main course at dinner.

Makes 4-5 dozen   **Difficulty level 2**

1/2	lb Napa cabbage	1	pkg dumpling wrappers
1	lb raw shrimp, shelled & deveined*	3	TBS salad oil
1	TBS cold water	1	cup chicken stock
1	TBS dry sherry		
1	TBS soy sauce		**CONDIMENTS:**
1	TBS sesame oil		1/4 cup soy sauce mixed
1	tsp salt		with 2 TBS vinegar
1	tsp minced ginger		hot chili sauce

1. In food processor with knife blade or manually with cleaver, chop cabbage into small pieces. Do not over chop or the filling will be too runny. Add shrimp and mix until chopped. Add next 6 ingredients and mix well.

2. Place 2 tsp filling in center of each wrapper. Wet edges with cold water. Fold the round in half forming a half-moon shape. Place dumplings on tray and cover with a dry towel.

3. Heat 2 TBS oil in non-stick 12" pan. Arrange dumplings in pan starting from center and radiating out like sun rays with sides of dumplings just touching. Cook over low heat until bottoms are lightly browned. Add chicken stock; cover pan and cook over medium heat, about 10 minutes, or until all liquid has evaporated. Uncover and drizzle remaining 1 TBS oil around edge of pan. Fry dumplings 1-2 minutes. Loosen dumplings from bottom of pan with a spatula. Place large serving plate over pan. Wearing rubber gloves to protect hands, quickly invert pan over sink. Serve dumplings fried side up with condiments.

* Ground meat such as pork, beef, chicken, or turkey may be substituted for shrimp.

虾 仁 梨 子

MINIATURE SHRIMP PEARS

Miniature shrimp pears make an exquisite appetizer. I like to serve them on special holidays and for formal dinner parties. Shrimp pears can be made ahead and fried, then frozen until ready to use. Reheat them on a cookie sheet in a 350° F oven for 10-15 minutes until crisp.

Makes about 30 pears   **Difficulty level 3**

1	lb raw shrimp, shelled & deveined	3	TBS cornstarch
1/2	cup water chestnuts	2	cups unseasoned dry bread crumbs
1	TBS vegetable shortening		
1	TBS dry sherry		parsley sprigs for garnish
2	tsp minced green onion	3	cups salad oil
2	tsp minced ginger root		
1	egg white, lightly beaten		CONDIMENTS:
1	tsp salt		plum sauce
1	tsp sesame oil		hot mustard sauce

1. In food processor with knife blade or manually with cleaver, mince shrimp, water chestnuts, and vegetable shortening. Add next 6 ingredients and mix thoroughly. Add cornstarch and blend well.

2. Shape 1 rounded tsp shrimp paste into a ball. Roll shrimp balls in bread crumbs. Gently form balls into a pear shape. Cut parsley sprigs into 1" sections. Place a sprig in center of top of each shrimp pear like a stem.

3. Heat oil to 350° F in wok over medium-high heat. Add shrimp pears, a few at a time, and fry until golden, about 2 minutes. Drain on paper towels. Arrange shrimp pears on a platter, and serve with condiments or eat as is.

SMOKED FISH

Although the traditional version of this dish is smoked, my mother always deep-fried the fish and served it cold. In fact, this dish is tastier the next day. It can be stored wrapped in the refrigerator for several days. Serve for a banquet or at a buffet.

Serves 6   **Difficulty level 3**

2	lb firm, white fish, cleaned with head and tail removed (carp, sea bass, red snapper, or pike)		
1/3	cup soy sauce	2 1/2	TBS dark brown sugar
2	TBS dry sherry	2	TBS chicken stock
4	slices ginger	3	cups salad oil
1	garlic clove, minced	1/2	tsp five spice powder
1	green onion, cut to 2" pieces	1/2	tsp sesame oil
1/2	tsp salt		

1. Wash fish and pat dry with paper towels. Split fish in half by cutting along backbone. Remove bones. Cut fish halves crosswise into ½" thick slices. In large bowl, mix next 6 ingredients. Add fish and toss gently. Marinate 2-3 hours at room temperature or overnight in refrigerator.

2. Remove fish slices from marinade with slotted spoon; reserve marinade. Drain fish thoroughly on a rack. Strain marinade through a sieve into a small saucepan, pressing down hard on ginger and green onions to extract all juices before discarding.

3. Bring marinade to a boil over high heat; reduce heat to low. Stir in brown sugar and chicken stock. Simmer while fish is frying.

4. Heat oil to 375° F in wok over medium-high heat. Fry fish about 6 pieces at a time, until crisp and dark brown. Dip in marinade and arrange on a serving platter. Cool fish to room temperature. Just before serving, sprinkle fish lightly with five spice powder and sesame oil. Serve cold.

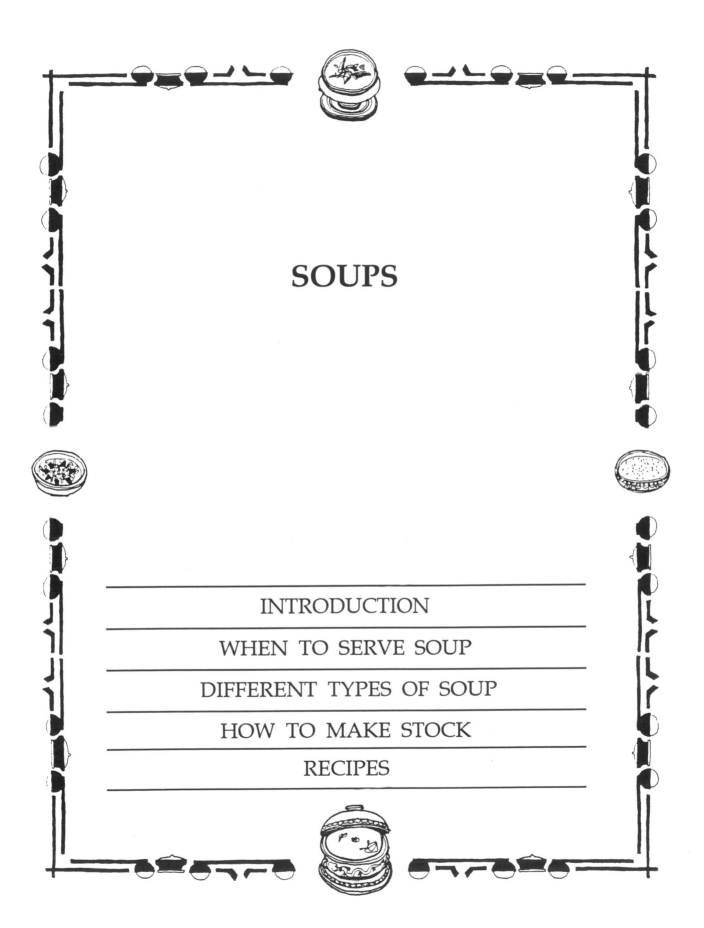

SOUPS

SOUPS

INTRODUCTION

Many Chinese serve soup with dinner. It is an excellent addition to any complete meal. In China, few people drink water, milk, cold drinks, wine, or alcohol with their meals except on special occasions. Thus, light and simple soups are needed to add more liquid to their diet.

Chinese soup has no cream or butter and therefore contains fewer calories. If you wish to lose weight, start each dinner with a bowl of light Chinese soup. The liquid fills you up and, at the same time, adds more vitamins and nutrients to your diet. For those who love soup and dislike vegetables, this is a good way to get more greens in the diet. Even if the vegetables in the soup are not eaten, many of the vitamins will be in the broth.

My family loves soup, and we have it everyday. It is as basic as rice with dinner and fruit for dessert. Most soups reheat well, so I often make a large pot and serve it for two days. When I have room in the freezer, I serve one batch and freeze the remaining for future use. With the microwave I can quickly warm any kind of soup. When I need to clean out my refrigerator, I utilize my leftovers to make a large pot of delicious soup.

WHEN TO SERVE SOUP

Most Westerners eat soup at the beginning of a meal, also as the main course of a meal. In China, soup is served throughout the meal. In fact, most Chinese prefer soup at the end of the meal, when one is most thirsty. At banquets, soup is served in the middle of the meal. Very expensive banquets might serve 2 or 3 different kinds of soup between courses. It is similar to the French serving sorbet between the seafood and the meat entrees.

DIFFERENT TYPES OF SOUP

Basically, there are 2 kinds of soup:

1. **Clear broth** — very light and delicate in flavor; and

2. **Thick soup** — usually thickened with cornstarch. An egg is often dropped in just before serving to add more body and texture.

The clear broth soup is served often in the Chinese meal because it cleans the palate and quenches the thirst. A good clear stock is a must to make any soup as tasty as possible.

HOW TO MAKE STOCK

To make a perfect pot of stock, always cook the stock slowly on low heat after the liquid comes to a boil. Do not let the stock boil too long, or the broth will become cloudy. Season the stock when ready to serve. Remove fat with a spoon, or put the stock in the refrigerator overnight. A layer of fat will solidify on top and can be easily lifted out.

Strain all the solids with a fine mesh strainer before storing. Pour into a covered container and refrigerate or freeze. Stock freezes well and will keep for a month. An ice tray can be used to freeze cubes of stock. After freezing, transfer them to a plastic bag. Whenever a recipe calls for 1 or 2 tablespoons of stock, simply use a frozen cube or two.

CHICKEN STOCK

Serves 6-8   **Difficulty level 1**

3	lbs stewing chicken or chicken parts (necks, gizzards, hearts, wings, backs, etc.)
2	slices ginger
2	green onions, cut in half
1	TBS dry sherry
10	cups water

1. Put all ingredients in a large pot. Bring to a boil over high heat. Immediately turn heat to low. Spoon residue from liquid. Simmer 2-3 hours.

2. Remove fat with a spoon. Strain stock through a fine strainer. This stock may be seasoned with salt and served as is or cooked with other ingredients for different kinds of soup.

OTHER INGREDIENTS: cucumber slices and tomato wedges
spinach leaves and tofu cubes
carrot and celery cubes

QUICK CHICKEN STOCK: If you do not have time to make chicken stock, canned "Swanson" clear chicken broth or "College Inn" both make a good substitute. These two brands are light and quite similar to Chinese chicken stock. If you use a canned broth, reduce salt in your cooking because it is already seasoned. You may also dilute canned broth by adding half as much water. The next best substitute is bouillon powder. This is richer and less salty than bouillon cubes.

EGG FLOWER SOUP

This is a basic Chinese soup. It is important to remove this delicate soup from heat immediately after you drop in the egg. Otherwise, the egg will coagulate.

Serves 4-6   **Difficulty level 1**

4	cups chicken stock	2	TBS minced ham
1	tsp salt	1	TBS minced green onion
1	slice ginger	1/2	tsp sesame oil
2	eggs	1/4	tsp black pepper
1/2	tsp dry sherry		

1. Put stock, salt, and ginger slice in a medium saucepan. Bring to a boil; remove ginger slice.*

2. Beat eggs and dry sherry slightly in a small bowl. Pour eggs slowly into boiling stock. Stir with chopsticks; immediately remove from heat. Garnish with minced ham, green onion, sesame oil, and black pepper. Serve hot.

* 1/4 cup diced tomatoes, peas, mushrooms, or celery may be added after stock comes to a boil. Return to a boil, and stir in beaten eggs.

MANDARIN CUCUMBER SOUP

The word Mandarin comes from the Northern part of China meaning Imperial China. It is often associated with light and delicate dishes. This soup is a perfect example of that region.

Serves 4-6   **Difficulty level 1**

1	medium-sized cucumber
1/4	cup thinly sliced, lean pork or beef
2	tsp soy sauce
1	tsp cornstarch
1/2	tsp dry sherry
4	cups chicken stock
1	tsp salt
1	tsp sesame oil

1. Peel cucumber, and cut lengthwise into 4 strips. Remove seeds. Cut into thin diagonal slices.

2. Mix meat slices with soy sauce, cornstarch, and dry sherry in a small bowl, and set aside.

3. Bring stock to a boil in a medium saucepan. Stir in meat mixture and cook until soup boils again. Add cucumber slices and salt. After cucumber softens, remove from heat. Garnish with sesame oil, and serve immediately.

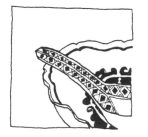

THREE FLAVORS SOUP

The combination of shrimp, water chestnuts, and snow peas makes this simple soup interesting in texture and delightful in flavor.

Serves 4-5   **Difficulty level 1**

1/4	lb raw, medium-sized shrimp	1	green onion, minced
8	water chestnuts or mushrooms	1	tsp salt
10	snow peas*	1/2	tsp sesame oil
4	cups chicken stock		dash of black pepper
1	slice ginger		

1. Wash, drain, and shell shrimp. With knife, butterfly and devein shrimp. Slice water chestnuts thinly crosswise. Snap off both ends of snow peas and remove strings. Wash and drain well. Cut snow peas in half on a diagonal.

2. Bring stock with a slice of ginger to a boil in a medium saucepan. Add green onion and water chestnuts. Add shrimp and salt. Add snow peas and let it come to a boil. Season with sesame oil and black pepper. Discard ginger and serve immediately.

* If snow peas are unavailable, substitute ⅓ bunch spinach leaves or ¼ cup peas.

西洋菜魚片湯

WATERCRESS AND FISH FILLET SOUP

The first time I had this soup was in my sister's house. I was pleasantly surprised at how refreshing and light this soup is.

Serves 6-8   **Difficulty level 1**

1/4	lb fresh, firm, white fish fillet (sea bass, sole, or perch)		
1	tsp cornstarch	2	tsp salt
1/2	tsp dry sherry	2	slices ginger
1/4	tsp salt	1/2	cup sliced mushrooms
6	oz watercress or spinach	1	tsp sesame oil
6	cups chicken stock	1/4	tsp black pepper

1. Cut fish into 2" x 1" x ¼" thick slices. Marinate fish with cornstarch, dry sherry, and ¼ tsp salt for 20 minutes at room temperature.

2. Rinse watercress or spinach, and cut into 1" long sections.

3. Bring stock to a boil in a large saucepan. Add 2 tsp salt, ginger, greens, and mushrooms. When liquid boils, add fish. Return soup to boiling. Season with sesame oil and black pepper. Serve immediately.

螺 肉 青 蒜 湯

CLAMS WITH GOLDEN MUSHROOMS SOUP

This soup can be cooked in a jiffy, and yet it is so delicious.

Serves 6-8   **Difficulty level 1**

6	cups chicken stock		1	TBS soy sauce
1	can (6 1/2 oz) chopped clams*		1	tsp salt
1/2	cup shredded carrots		1/4	tsp black pepper
1	oz golden mushrooms			
1/2	cup shredded green onions			

1. Heat stock in a large saucepan. Drain clams and add liquid to stock. Bring to a boil.

2 Add shredded carrots and mushrooms; cook for 3 minutes over medium heat. Add seafood and green onions.

3. Season with soy sauce and salt. Return soup to boiling. Sprinkle with black pepper. Serve immediately.

* Many kinds of canned seafood may be used, such as crab meat, shrimp, lobster, smoked oysters, or smoked clams.

白菜豆腐湯

BOK CHOY AND TOFU SOUP

This is a fast and flavorful soup which is perfect with any meal.

Serves 5-6   **Difficulty level 1**

1/2	lb Bok Choy or fresh spinach
1/2	lb regular tofu
5	cups chicken stock
2	TBS minced ham or mushrooms
1	tsp salt
1	tsp sesame oil
1/4	tsp black pepper

1. Wash and remove hard stems from vegetable. Cut into 1" sections. Drain and cut tofu into ½" cubes.

2. Heat stock to boiling in a large saucepan. Add vegetable and tofu. Boil for a few minutes. Season with ham, salt, sesame oil, and pepper. Serve hot.

蟹肉菠菜湯

CRAB AND SPINACH SOUP

When my son was a baby, I cooked this soup for him often because it is high in protein and rich in calcium. This delicious and nutritious soup can be served as a main course with sesame bread.

Serves 6-8   **Difficulty level 2**

2	TBS salad oil	4	cups chicken stock*
2	tsp salt	1	cup diced firm tofu
1	slice ginger root	3	TBS cornstarch mixed
1/2	cup crab meat		with 1/2 cup chicken stock
1	tsp dry sherry	1	egg, beaten
1/3	bunch spinach, washed & chopped		

1. Heat oil in a large saucepan over medium heat. Season oil with salt and ginger. Stir in crab meat and sherry. Add spinach and cook until wilted.

2. Add stock, and heat to boiling. Add tofu, and stir in cornstarch mixture. As soon as soup boils again, stir in egg. Remove from heat immediately. Serve hot.

* 1 can (14 1/2oz) chicken broth with 2 cups of water may be used instead of 4 cups of chicken stock.

白菜 細粉湯

NAPA CABBAGE AND BEAN THREAD SOUP

Children love to eat bean threads because they are slippery and look like transparent noodles. Bean threads must be added at the last minute of cooking, otherwise they will absorb all the liquid.

Serves 6-8   **Difficulty level 2**

1/4	cup dried shrimp or ham	2	slices ginger
3	TBS cold water	6	cups chicken stock
1	tsp dry sherry	1 1/2	tsp salt
2	oz bean thread	1/4	tsp black pepper
1	lb Napa cabbage	1/2	tsp sesame oil
2	TBS salad oil		

1. Soak dried shrimp in cold water and dry sherry in a small bowl; set aside.

2. Soak bean thread in warm water for 10 minutes. Use scissors to cut threads into 6"-8" lengths. Rinse and drain well.

3. Wash Napa cabbage and cut into 1½" pieces.

4. Heat oil in a large saucepan over medium heat. Add ginger and cabbage. Stir and cook until cabbage is wilted. Add dried shrimp mixture with all ingredients except bean thread and sesame oil. Bring to a boil. Cover and simmer until cabbage is transparent and tender. Add bean thread. Return soup to boiling. Remove from heat and garnish with sesame oil. Serve immediately.

SPINACH VELVET SOUP

My parents came from a small town in China called Ninpo, where thick and hearty soups are often served. For a simplified version of this soup, please read the note at the end of this recipe.

Serves 8   **Difficulty level 2**

12	oz fresh spinach	4	TBS cornstarch mixed
2	TBS sugar		with 1/2 cup chicken stock
3	egg whites	2	TBS salad oil
1	TBS cold water	2	tsp salt
5 1/2	cups chicken stock	1	tsp sesame oil
2	TBS minced Smithfield ham or prosciutto		

1. Remove tough stems from spinach leaves. Rinse leaves until thoroughly free of grit.

2. Fill large saucepan halfway with water; add sugar. Bring to a boil over high heat. Add spinach, stirring gently, until water returns to boiling. Drain immediately. Rinse under running cold water until cold; drain again. Squeeze as much liquid as possible from spinach. Mince spinach; set aside.

3. Beat egg whites and water in small bowl with fork until blended but not foamy; set aside.

4. Heat stock to boiling in the same saucepan over high heat. Add 1 TBS ham; reduce heat to medium. Simmer uncovered for 5 minutes. Stir in cornstarch mixture in slow, steady stream. Continue to stir until soup is thickened and clear, about 30 seconds. Stir in salad oil.

5. Increase heat to high; stir in spinach. Heat soup to boiling; then remove from heat. Hold bowl containing egg white mixture about 6" above soup; stirring soup gently, add egg whites in slow, steady stream. Let stand without stirring 30 seconds; then stir to distribute egg white strands. Stir

in salt and sesame oil. Pour soup into warmed tureen; sprinkle with remaining 1 TBS ham. Serve hot.

EASY SHORT CUT: Use 1 large can (49 ½ oz) chicken broth for stock. Reduce salt to 1 tsp. Substitute a thawed 10 oz box of frozen chopped spinach for fresh spinach. Squeeze out all the liquid, skipping steps 1 and 2. Start with step 3.

STEAMED EGG SOUP

The texture of this soup will be smooth and custard-like only if the air content is kept to a minimum. For this reason the eggs should not be over beaten. Steam over low heat. Too much heat will cause the eggs to separate and form holes in the surface of the custard.

Serves 4   **Difficulty level 2**

3   eggs
1   can (14 1/2 oz) chicken broth
1/2   tsp dry sherry
1   TBS minced green onion
dash of soy sauce

1. Beat eggs lightly in a bowl. Add chicken broth and dry sherry. Mix well. Pour into 4 rice bowls.

2. Place bowls on rack in wok or steamer over 3 cups of COLD water. Cover and steam on medium-high heat until water comes to a boil; then reduce heat to medium-low and steam until eggs are firm, about 5-10 minutes. Check with a toothpick or knife to see if the eggs are done. If they are still runny, steam a few minutes longer.

3. Garnish with minced green onion, season lightly with soy sauce, and serve hot.

鍋 巴 湯

SIZZLING RICE SOUP

In order for the rice to sizzle, the soup has to be piping hot and the rice patties very crisp.

Serves 4-6   **Difficulty level 3**

2	cups cooked short grain rice	**SEASONING SAUCE:**
1/4	lb raw, medium-sized shrimp	1 tsp cornstarch
1/2	lb Napa cabbage	1 tsp soy sauce
4	cups chicken stock	1/2 tsp salt
1/2	cup peas	1/4 tsp sugar
1/4	cup sliced mushrooms	dash of pepper
2	cups salad oil	
1	tsp minced green onion	
1/2	tsp sesame oil	

1. Preheat oven to 300°F. Press cooked rice into a thin layer (no more than ¼" thick) on a baking sheet. Bake for 30 minutes. Turn rice, and bake for another 30 minutes. Remove from oven. When cool enough to handle, break into 2" patties.*

2. Wash, drain, and shell shrimp. With knife, butterfly and devein shrimp. Marinate shrimp with seasoning sauce in a bowl for 15 minutes at room temperature.

3. Wash and cut cabbage into 1" pieces.

4. Bring stock to a boil in a medium saucepan over high heat. Add shrimp, cabbage, peas, and mushrooms. Return to a boil.

5. Meanwhile, heat oil in wok to 325°F over medium-high heat. Fry rice patties until golden brown, about 5 minutes. Drain on paper towels.

6. Pour hot soup into a preheated tureen. Garnish with green onion and sesame oil. Immediately add rice patties to soup at the table. Serve at once.

Rice patties may be baked in advance, stored in an airtight container, and refrigerated or frozen. Fry patties just before serving.

仄茄玉米湯

TOMATO WITH SWEET CORN SOUP

This soup is served often at banquets. Because fresh corn is not readily available in China, this soup is considered a very special treat.

Serves 6-8   **Difficulty level 2**

1	egg white	1	cup diced tomatoes
2	TBS milk	1/3	cup green peas
6	cups chicken stock	2	tsp salt
1	can (8 3/4 oz) creamed corn	4	TBS cornstarch mixed with 4 TBS water
1/2	cup sliced mushrooms	1	TBS chopped cooked ham

1. Beat egg white with a fork until frothy in a small bowl. Beat in milk and set aside.

2 Bring stock to a boil in a large saucepan. Add corn and mix well. Return mixture to a boil.

3. Add mushrooms, tomatoes, peas, and salt; return to a boil. Reduce heat to low; slowly stir in cornstarch mixture until thickened. Turn off heat and immediately pour in egg white mixture, stirring only once. Garnish with chopped ham. Serve hot.

酸 辣 湯

HOT AND SOUR SOUP

Hot and Sour Soup is the most popular soup in the Northern part of China. Medical studies indicate that the black fungus helps in lowering blood pressure and the golden needle is rich in iron and vitamin C.

Serves 6-8   **Difficulty level 3**

1/4	cup pork or chicken, shredded	1/2	cup shredded tofu
1	tsp cornstarch	2 1/2	TBS cornstarch mixed
1	tsp dry sherry		with 1/2 cup water
1/4	cup dried black fungus*	1	egg, beaten
1/4	cup dried golden needles*	1 1/2	TBS dark rice vinegar*
3 1/2	cups chicken stock	1/2	tsp white pepper
1	TBS soy sauce	1	TBS minced green onion
1 1/2	tsp salt	1	tsp sesame oil

1. Mix shredded meat, cornstarch, and sherry in a small bowl.

2. Soak black fungus and golden needles in separate bowls in hot water for 10 minutes. Wash and drain well. Cut off stems from black fungus and golden needles. Cut black fungus into small pieces; cut golden needles in half.

3. Put stock, soy sauce, and salt into a medium saucepan. Bring to a boil and stir in marinated meat. Boil for 1 minute. Add black fungus and golden needles; boil for 1 minute. Add tofu. When soup boils again, stir in cornstarch mixture until thickened. Mix in beaten egg and remove from heat immediately. Pour soup into a large tureen.

4. Stir vinegar and pepper into soup. Garnish with green onion and sesame oil. Serve hot.

* Chinese black mushrooms may be substituted for black fungus and bamboo shoots for golden needles. If you cannot obtain dark rice vinegar, use cider vinegar or rice vinegar instead.

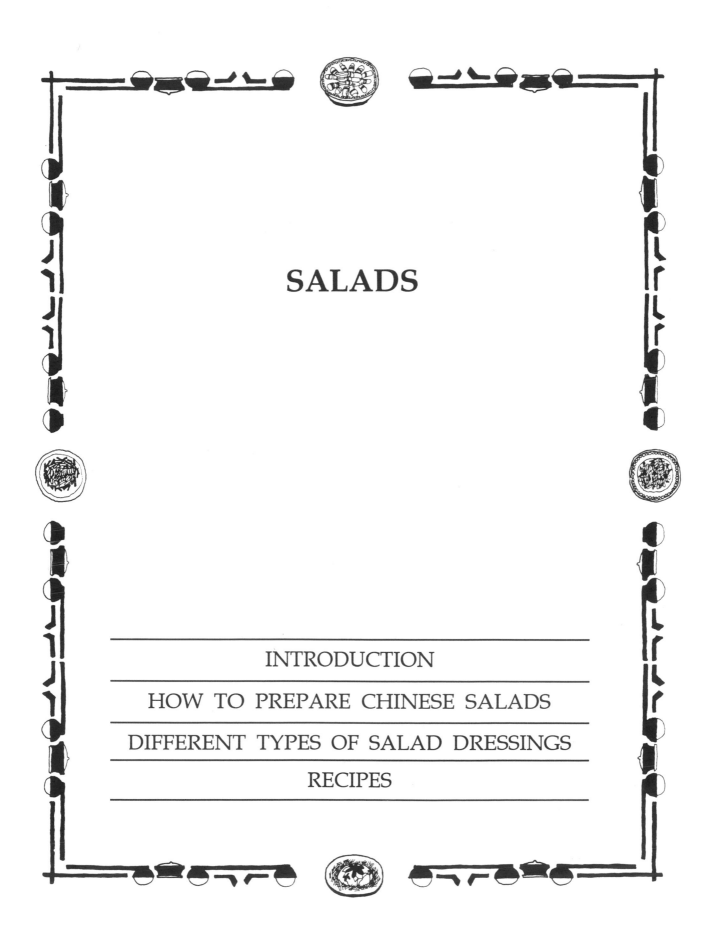

SALADS

INTRODUCTION

HOW TO PREPARE CHINESE SALADS

DIFFERENT TYPES OF SALAD DRESSINGS

RECIPES

SALADS

INTRODUCTION

Salads of raw vegetables are not often served in China because Chinese people are concerned about the safety of eating raw food. Most vegetables in Chinese salads are peeled, blanched, parboiled, or pickled before being served as a cold dish. At banquets, the salads are presented as part of a cold platter.

With increased awareness of the nutritious value of fresh vegetables, salad has become an important part in everyone's diet. Today's time-conscious cook will find salads quick and easy to prepare. This chapter includes many "salad favorites" of my family and my students.

HOW TO PREPARE CHINESE SALADS

The most important thing to remember when you are fixing salads is to wash your hands and equipment very well. Many people get sick from eating salads that are not prepared properly. Since the vegetables are usually raw, bacteria and germs have a greater chance to grow.

Salad vegetables, like cucumber and tomato, are often peeled. A very easy way to peel a tomato is to blanch it in boiling water for a minute and then rinse with cold water. The skin can be easily peeled off.

Many salads are salted first. It is a good idea to use kosher salt or non-iodized salt. The vegetable will stay crisp and keep fresh longer. By salting the vegetable first, more liquid is removed, and thus the salad dressing is absorbed better.

Some vegetables taste better after soaking in ice water. This is especially true of celery and carrots. Again, they are always washed and peeled in China. To retain more vitamins, you may leave the skin on and use a brush to remove all the dirt.

Several vegetables need to be blanched first before being tossed with a salad dressing. Asparagus and bean sprouts taste better after being blanched. The bitterness of asparagus and the nutty flavor of bean sprouts will be removed by blanching, but take care to preserve crispness by rinsing immediately with cold water after blanching. Otherwise, the heat in the vegetables will continue to cook and soften them. Drain blanched vegetables thoroughly before tossing with salad dressing.

Pickling is a popular method of preserving in China and adds flavor to salads. Most pickled vegetables taste better after being marinated for a day or two. Some vegetables take as long as one week. Always pickle in sterilized glass jars, and keep pickled vegetables in the refrigerator. Vegetables can be pickled ahead in large quantities and are favorites at buffets and picnics.

DIFFERENT TYPES OF SALAD DRESSING

There are two basic types of salad dressing in China:

1. Soy sauce with sesame seed oil (fewer calories); and

2. Sweet and sour dressing with equal amounts of sugar and vinegar.

Sometimes hot chili oil, hot pepper sauce, or dried red chili peppers are added to give a more spicy flavor. You can add or omit them to suit your own taste.

The salad dressings are interchangeable. For example, the Cucumber and Tomato Salad may be sweet and sour or seasoned with soy sauce and sesame oil. The same applies to other salad dishes. You may use the sweet and sour dressing from the Crispy Salad recipe on page 110 for any of your favorite salads. Double the dressing and keep it in a glass jar in your refrigerator. This way you will always have an Oriental salad dressing at your finger tips.

三然凉拌

CARROT, CUCUMBER, AND DAIKON SALAD

The delightful combination of these three vegetables makes this salad look appealingly light and colorful.

Serves 6 **Difficulty Level 1**

2 cups finely shredded daikon	**DRESSING:**
1 cup finely shredded carrot	2 TBS cider vinegar
1 cup finely shredded cucumber	1 TBS sugar
1 TBS non-iodized salt	1 tsp sesame oil

1. Mix vegetables with salt. Marinate for ½ hour at room temperature.

2. Mix dressing ingredients in a small bowl and set aside.

3. Rinse vegetables lightly with cold water to remove excess salt; drain well. Add dressing and toss. Serve cold.

黄瓜番茄

CUCUMBER AND TOMATO SALAD

My friends always ask me for this simple recipe. The red and green color combination makes it a favorite salad to serve during the holidays.

Serves 3-4 **Difficulty level 1**

1	**cucumber***
1	**large tomato***
1/2	**tsp non-iodized salt**

<u>DRESSING</u>:

1	**TBS sugar**
1	**TBS cider vinegar**
1	**tsp sesame oil**

1. Peel cucumber and cut lengthwise into 4 strips. Remove seeds. Cut into 3/4" cubes.

2. Pour boiling water over tomato. Let sit for a minute in hot water. Rinse well in cold water; peel. Cut into sections. Remove seeds by scraping away with a knife tip. Cut into 3/4" cubes.

3. Mix cucumber and tomato; add salt. Toss lightly. Cover and store in refrigerator until ready to serve.

4. When ready to eat, drain off excess liquid. Mix dressing ingredients in a small bowl. Pour dressing over salad, toss, and serve cold.

** Radishes and celery slices may be substituted for cucumber and tomato. If using a Japanese cucumber (also called English, Hothouse, Burpless, or seedless cucumber), do not peel. Simply remove the plastic wrap, wash, and dice.*

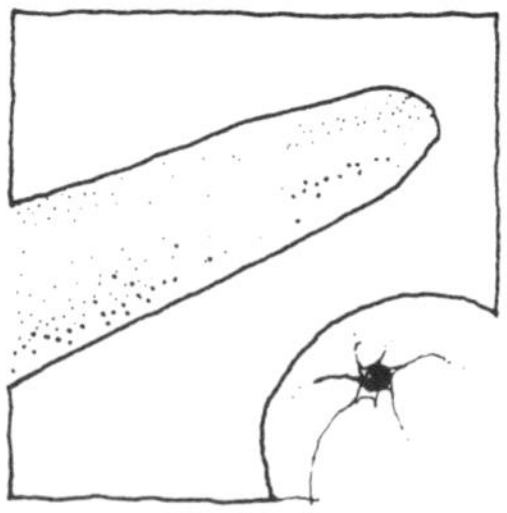

冷拌芹菜

CELERY AND CARROT SALAD

This is a refreshing salad. It may be served with the sweet and sour dressing on page 98.

Serves 4-6 **Difficulty level 1**

1/2	large bunch celery without leaves, finely shredded
1	carrot, finely shredded
1	TBS ginger, peeled and finely shredded (optional)
2	tsp non-iodized salt

DRESSING:

2	TBS soy sauce
1	tsp sesame oil

1. Soak celery, carrot, and ginger shreds in ice water with salt for ½ hour at room temperature (not more than 1 hour), and drain well. Cover and store in refrigerator until ready to serve.

2. Mix dressing ingredients in a small bowl and set aside.

3. When ready to eat, lightly toss vegetables with dressing.*
   Serve immediately.

* ½ cup cooked shredded chicken breast or ham may be added for more flavor.

菠 辣 黄 瓜

HOT AND SOUR CUCUMBER SALAD

If you like garlic, you will love this spicy salad. For best results, prepare this salad the day before.

Serves 6   **Difficulty level 1**

| 1 1/3 | lb small pickle cucumbers |
| 1 | TBS non-iodized salt |

DRESSING:

1	TBS chopped garlic
1	TBS sesame oil
2	tsp sugar
2	tsp white vinegar
1/2	tsp hot pepper sauce

1. Wash and cut off ends of cucumber. Do not peel. Cut into bite-sized pieces. Mix with salt in a bowl, and marinate for ½ hour at room temperature. Rinse lightly with cold water and drain.

2. Mix dressing ingredients in a small bowl and pour over cucumbers. Toss to mix well. Refrigerate for 6 hours or overnight. Serve cold.

FRESH ASPARAGUS SALAD

In Spring, when asparagus is at its best, this is the perfect salad to serve.

Serves 4-6   **Difficulty level 1**

1 1/2-2 lb fresh asparagus	**DRESSING:**
1 tomato	**4 tsp soy sauce**
	2 tsp sesame oil
	1 tsp sugar

1. Bend asparagus stalks back until tough root end snaps off. Discard ends. Slice stalks into 1½" lengths, using rolling cut method (page 46) (about 3 cups of asparagus pieces).

2. Wash asparagus under running cold water; parboil by dropping into 8 cups of rapidly boiling water for 1 minute. Drain at once and rinse thoroughly with cold water to stop cooking and set color. Drain well. Cut tomato in half and slice.

3. In a salad bowl, combine dressing ingredients and mix until the sugar is completely dissolved. Add asparagus. With a large spoon, toss to coat each asparagus piece thoroughly with dressing. Chill slightly, about ½ hour before serving. Garnish with tomato slices.

涼拌白蘿蔔

SHREDDED DAIKON WITH CILANTRO

There is an old saying in China, "When the turnips are ripe, the doctors cry." This is because turnips or daikons are high in fiber and nutrients.

Serves 6   **Difficulty level 1**

1	lb daikon
1	tsp non-iodized salt
1/4	cup chopped cilantro
1	TBS soy sauce

Cilantro leaves for garnish

DRESSING:

1	TBS white vinegar
1	tsp sugar
1	tsp sesame oil

1. Wash, peel, and finely shred daikon. Mix with salt in a bowl and marinate for ½ hour at room temperature. Rinse lightly with cold water and drain well.

2. Mix dressing ingredients in a small bowl and pour over daikon. Add chopped cilantro; toss lightly.

3. When ready to eat, season with soy sauce and garnish with cilantro leaves.

萝卜熟医生哭

BEAN SPROUTS SALAD WITH HAM GARNISH

Bean sprouts are nutritious and economical. They are high in protein, especially when they are eaten with rice.

Serves 4-5   **Difficulty level 1**

1	**lb raw bean sprouts, about 4 cups tightly packed**
1/4	**cup finely shredded ham***

DRESSING:

2	**TBS soy sauce**
1	**tsp sesame oil**

1. Wash and remove tails of bean sprouts. In a large saucepan, heat 10 cups of water to boiling. Add bean sprouts. Just before water boils again, remove pan from heat. Pour bean sprouts into a colander; drain. Rinse thoroughly with cold water until cold. Drain well.

2. Place drained bean sprouts in a large salad bowl and add ham. Cover and store in refrigerator until ready to serve.

3. Mix dressing ingredients in a small bowl and set aside.

4. When ready to eat, toss bean sprouts and ham with dressing.

* ¼ cup shredded, cooked chicken or smoked turkey may be substituted for ham. ¼ cup shredded snow peas, celery, or carrots may be parboiled and added to the salad for additional color.

蟹 肉 拌 黄 瓜

CRAB MEAT AND CUCUMBER SALAD

Crab is in season in summertime. This salad can be served as a light main course for lunch.

Serves 4-6   **Difficulty level 1**

2	medium-sized cucumbers
1/2	lb fresh crab meat or
	1 can (7 1/2 oz) crab meat
1	TBS minced green onion
1	tomato, sliced

DRESSING:
2	TBS white vinegar
2	TBS soy sauce
1	TBS sesame oil
1	tsp sugar
1/8	tsp white pepper

1. Peel cucumbers and cut lengthwise into 4 strips. Remove seeds. Cut into 2" shreds.

2. Pick over crab meat and discard shell and cartilage.

3. Mix dressing ingredients in a medium bowl. Add shredded cucumbers and crab meat. Toss to coat and chill slightly, no more than an hour.

4. When ready to serve, arrange cucumber on a serving plate. Sprinkle with green onion and garnish with tomato slices.

洋菜拌黃瓜

AGAR AGAR SALAD WITH SPICY DRESSING

Agar agar has a wonderful texture. It resembles icicles and is always a conversation piece.

Serves 4   **Difficulty level 1**

1	medium-sized cucumber
1	cup agar agar*
1/4	cup finely shredded carrots

DRESSING:

1	TBS sugar
1	TBS white vinegar
2	tsp sesame oil
1	tsp soy sauce
1/2	tsp salt
1/4	tsp hot pepper sauce

1. Peel cucumber and cut lengthwise into 4 strips. Remove seeds. Cut diagonally into ¼" slices.

2. Cut agar agar with scissors into 1" lengths. Soften in cold water for 5 to 10 minutes. Drain well.

3. Mix dressing ingredients in a large bowl. Add cucumber, agar agar, and carrots. Toss with a large spoon to coat. Chill before serving.

* ½ lb parboiled bean sprouts may be substituted for agar agar.

冷拌辣蜇皮

SPICY JELLYFISH SALAD

Jellyfish is considered an exotic dish in China. It is often served at banquets, especially during celebrations like Chinese New Year. The crunchy texture with spicy dressing makes this salad surprisingly delicious.

Serves 4-5   **Difficulty level 2**

3	**oz salted jellyfish**
1/2	**cup shredded cucumber**
1/2	**cup shredded daikon***
Cilantro leaves for garnish	

DRESSING:

1	**TBS soy sauce**
1	**TBS sesame oil**
1	**tsp cider vinegar**
1	**tsp chopped garlic**
1/2	**tsp salt**
1/2	**tsp sugar**
1/4	**tsp black pepper**

1. Rinse jellyfish and shred. Soak in warm water to cover for 30 minutes; drain. Soak in cold water to cover for 1 or more hours until softened, changing water several times to remove salt. Drain well.

2. Rinse shredded cucumber and daikon in cold water; drain.

3. Mix dressing ingredients in a small bowl and set aside.

4. Arrange cucumber and daikon shreds on a serving plate. Top with jellyfish. Pour dressing over salad; toss lightly just before serving. Garnish with cilantro leaves.

* ½ cup shredded celery, carrots, or napa cabbage may be substituted for the above vegetables.

PICKLED VEGETABLES, CANTONESE STYLE

Cantonese often serve this salad as an appetizer. These pickled vegetables will keep several days in the refrigerator. In fact, the longer they are pickled, the better they taste.

Serves 4-6   **Difficulty level 2**

1/4	lb daikon, turnip, or white radish
1	stalk celery*
1/2	large carrot
1/2	red pepper
5	slices peeled ginger
1/2	TBS non-iodized salt

DRESSING:
3	TBS white vinegar
3	TBS sugar

1. Peel daikon, celery, and carrot. Cut red peppers in half and remove seeds. Cut vegetables into bite-sized pieces.

2. Mix vegetables, ginger slices, and salt in a large bowl and marinate for ½ hour at room temperature. Rinse with cold water; drain and pat dry with paper towel.

3. Mix vinegar and sugar in a small bowl until sugar dissolves. Pour vinegar mixture over vegetables; toss to mix well. Let stand 6 hours in refrigerator. Serve cold.

* 1 small pickling cucumber may be substituted for celery.

凉 拌 西 洋 菜

WATERCRESS AND WATER CHESTNUT SALAD

Watercress belongs to the mustard family of plants and has a pungent taste. When cooking watercress, always do so quickly in order to destroy its bitter taste.

Serves 4-5   **Difficulty level 2**

2	bunches watercress
8	water chestnuts
3	oz baked savory tofu
	or 1 cup canned mushrooms

DRESSING:

2	tsp soy sauce
2	tsp sesame oil
1	tsp sugar
1/4	tsp salt

1. Trim and discard tough ends of the watercress stems. Wash under cold running water. In a large saucepan, heat 10 cups of water to boiling. Add watercress. Bring to a boil; remove pan from heat. Pour watercress into a colander; drain. Rinse thoroughly with cold water until cold. Drain well and pat dry with paper towels. With a cleaver, chop watercress finely.

2. Wash and drain water chestnuts. Cut into ⅛" slices and chop finely. Chop tofu into fine pieces.

3. Mix dressing ingredients in a large bowl. Add watercress, water chestnuts, and tofu. Toss until well coated with dressing. Serve chilled.

拌 干 丝

TOFU SPAGHETTI AND CELERY SALAD

Tofu spaghetti is high in calcium and low in calories. This salad is similar to cold pasta dishes.

Serves 4   **Difficulty level 2**

1	cup finely shredded celery
1/4	cup finely shredded carrot
1	tsp baking soda
1	pkg (6 oz) tofu spaghetti*
lettuce leaves for garnish	

DRESSING:

1	TBS sesame oil
1/2	TBS soy sauce
1/2	tsp salt
1/4	tsp hot pepper sauce

1. Heat 10 cups of water to boiling in a large saucepan. Add celery and carrot. Return to boiling. Remove vegetables with a strainer and rinse with cold water until cold. Drain well.

2. In the same pot of boiling water, add baking soda and tofu. Turn off heat and soak tofu in hot water until soft, about 5 minutes. Stir lightly to separate tofu spaghetti. Drain and rinse with cold water. Pat dry with paper towels.

3. Mix dressing ingredients in a medium bowl. Add vegetables and tofu. Toss lightly with dressing. Serve cold on a platter garnished with lettuce leaves.

*Firm tofu may be substituted for tofu spaghetti. To remove excess moisture from tofu, place tofu on paper towels. Place a cutting board directly above tofu. Put a pot of water on top of the board for about an hour. Then cut into thin strips. Skip step 2.

洋菜怂

CRISPY SALAD WITH PUFFED RICE STICKS

This is my students' favorite salad. Crispy Salad with Puffed Rice Sticks is almost a meal in itself, especially when it is served with sesame bread.

Serves 6-8   **Difficulty level 3**

2	oz medium-sized rice sticks*	
2-3	cups salad oil	
1	medium-sized head of lettuce, shredded	
1/2	lb cooked shrimp, crab meat, or shredded chicken	
4	green onions, shredded	
2	TBS chopped toasted almonds	
2	TBS white sesame seeds	

DRESSING:

1/4	cup virgin olive oil
3	TBS cider vinegar
2	TBS sugar
1	TBS sesame oil
1	tsp salt
1/2	tsp freshly ground pepper

1. Break rice sticks into pieces. Heat oil to 375°F in wok. Drop a few strands into oil; these should puff and turn white immediately. Fry in batches over medium-high heat until all puffed. Drain on paper towels.

2. Mix dressing ingredients in measuring cup and set aside.

3. Place remaining salad ingredients and puffed rice sticks in a large bowl. Add dressing <u>just before serving</u> and toss lightly. Serve immediately. Rice sticks become soft if salad is tossed early.

* Rice sticks may be fried and stored in a plastic bag overnight.

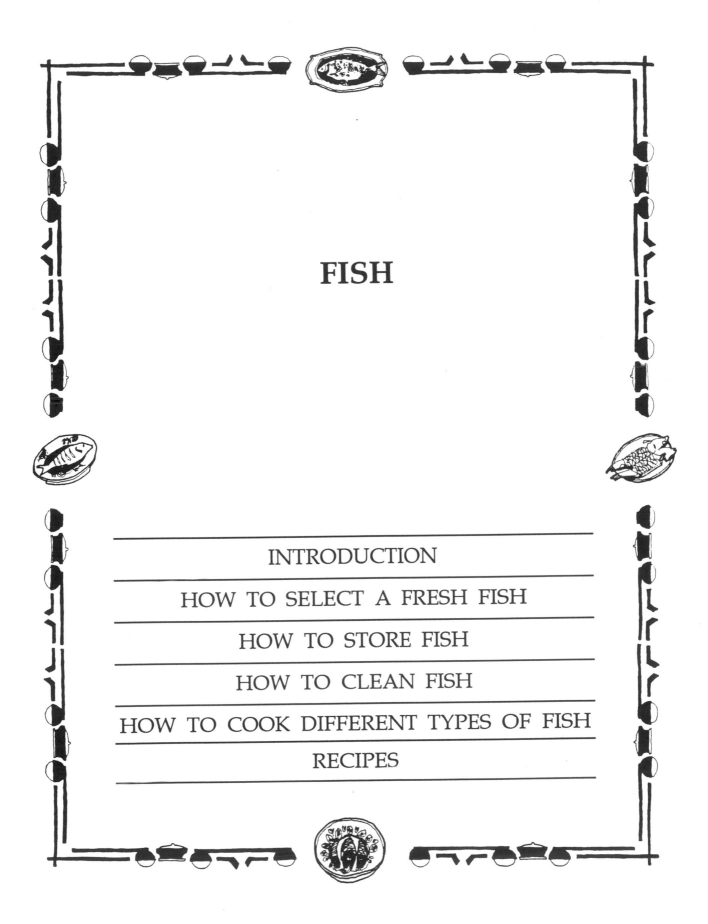

FISH

FISH

INTRODUCTION

Fish is very nutritious—it is high in protein, low in fat and cholesterol. In China, fish is eaten almost daily and is usually cheaper than meat. The Chinese character for fish is "Yu." It has the same sound as another "Yu" meaning abundance or prosperity. This is why fish is always served on special occasions, such as New Year's or at banquets.

The Chinese have been eating fish for almost 5,000 years. China has 3,000 miles of coastline and many lakes and rivers where fresh water fish multiply. Fish breeding ponds have been in use for centuries. Chinese like to eat all types of fish. The fresher the fish, the better it is. In China you will see live fish being sold in the markets. Restaurants in China, famous for seafood, all have tanks with live fish and shellfish for the diners' choice.

In China, fish is often served whole. In fact, many Chinese consider the head the best part of the fish. There is a famous dish in Taiwan where only fish heads, cooked in a delightful brown sauce, are served to each guest.

Scientists have discovered many nutrients in the skin of fish. By cooking fish whole, more nutrients are retained, and the fish is juicier and more tender.

In addition to recipes for whole fish, I have included, in this chapter, many fillet dishes which are easier to prepare and eat.

HOW TO SELECT FRESH FISH

When selecting fish, look for the following (refer to chart on next page):

1. The skin must be smooth and moist, not sticky or dry.

2. The flesh should be firm and springy with no blemishes.

3. Tug at the scales. If scales are loose, the fish is not fresh.

4. The eyes should be bright and clean, full and not sunken.

5. Lift the gills to see if the color underneath is bright red indicating freshness.

6. The aroma of fish should be pleasant and not smell of decay.

7. Fresh fish should have a "still alive" appearance.

CHART OF A FRESH FISH

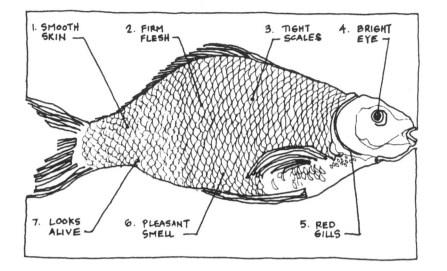

1. SMOOTH SKIN
2. FIRM FLESH
3. TIGHT SCALES
4. BRIGHT EYE
5. RED GILLS
6. PLEASANT SMELL
7. LOOKS ALIVE

HOW TO STORE FISH

Fish is extremely perishable so refrigerate it immediately after you return from shopping. Store in the coldest part of the refrigerator, packed in ice and try to cook fish within 24 hours of purchase. If fish is frozen, defrost in the refrigerator before using, or in running cold water. Never refreeze thawed fish.

HOW TO CLEAN FISH

Most seafood markets will clean fish for you. But you can quickly learn to clean fish yourself. If you fish or buy imported frozen fish, you will need to know how to clean fish. Below are three easy steps:

1. Scaling — Use a cleaver or large spoon to scrape off scales in short strokes. To prevent scales from flying everywhere, place the fish in a sink filled with a few inches of cold water. Work from tail to head.

2. Gutting — Cut along the belly of the fish between the anal fin and head. Cut the innards loose from the gills and pull out the gut and other organs. Be very careful not to break the gall bladder, a small yellowish blue sack, that tastes bitter. Remove the gills by pulling them out from the gill openings. Wash gutted fish with cold water to remove the blood. Drain and dry with paper towel.

3. Scoring — Make several diagonal cuts across the body, almost touching the bone on both sides of the fish. Make cuts about 1" apart and ¼" to ½" deep. Do this to ensure even cooking.

HOW TO CLEAN FISH IN 3 EASY STEPS

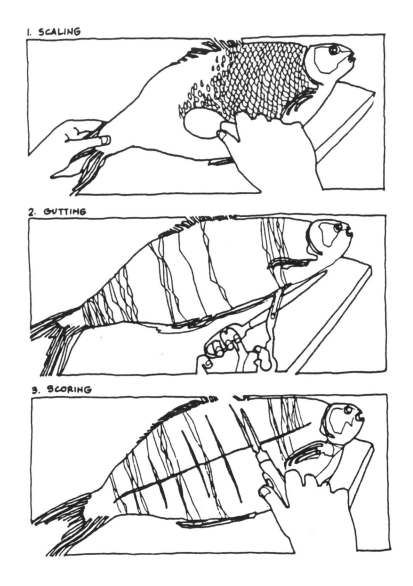

HOW TO COOK DIFFERENT TYPES OF FISH

The most important thing to remember in cooking fish is do not overcook. Overcooking turns fish dry, tough, rubbery, and flavorless. Pierce the thickest part of the fish with chopsticks or a fork to test for doneness. Fish flakes easily when it is cooked.

The wok is a perfect pot for cooking fish. Heat the wok to the smoking point before adding oil. This way, the fish will not stick to the wok. This step is especially critical when cooking a whole fish with the skin on.

Always serve fish as soon as possible after cooking. Do not reheat. However, some methods of cooking, smoking and braising for example, make fish taste good hot or cold.

Recognize the type of fish you have purchased before you decide which cooking method to use. Basically there are three main types of fish: those low in fat, fish that are moderately fatty, and those high in fat. Usually the color of the flesh indicates fat content: the lighter the meat, the lower the fat, and vice versa. See the chart below for examples.

Type of Fish	Kinds of Fish	Methods of Cooking
1. Low fat fish: White or very light colored flesh	sole, sturgeon, cod, sea bass, flounder, perch, pike, kingfish, etc.	stir-fry deep-fry stew
2. Moderately fatty fish: tan or light brown flesh	blue fish, carp, catfish, mullet, swordfish, trout, etc.	braise steam poach
3. Fish with high oil content: deep pink flesh	mackerel, salmon, smelt etc.	bake smoke

There are many cooking methods for fish:

1. STIR-FRY — This method of cooking requires some skill in handling the fish fillet. First, select a firm, white fish. Cut into bite-sized pieces. Marinate fish with seasoning and cornstarch. Then partially cook it in a large quantity of medium-hot oil. This seals in flavor and juices while giving the fish a velvety finish. Finally, stir-fry fish lightly with the other ingredients. Different sauces may be added to the fish while stir-frying.

2. DEEP-FRY — Many recipes call for whole fish. The skin and the bones of the fish become so crispy after frying that these become delicious to eat also. The fish is usually marinated with salt and wine, then coated with cornstarch to hold it together, and finally fried on both sides to a crisp. Be very careful not to tear or break the skin. Serve with a sauce poured on top. The best kinds of fish for frying are flounder, smelt, kingfish, and other small fish. To deep-fry fish fillets, use the same firm, white fish as for stir-frying. Often fillets are coated with a batter, then fried in a large pot of hot oil until golden brown. A sauce may be served as a dip or stir-fried lightly with the fish.

3. BRAISE — Usually large, whole fish are cooked using this method. Catfish, kingfish, rock cod, or any other firm fish may be used. First the fish is sealed and browned in oil. Then it is cooked in sauce for 5 to 10 minutes. The fish becomes very flavorful and can be served cold. Braising is a popular cooking method in China.

4. **STEAM** — Use only very fresh fish for steamed dishes. Do not steam frozen fish. The best types of fish to steam are fish with a moderate fat content. First marinate the fish in salt and wine to remove any fishy smell. Place on a serving plate and add seasonings. Steam over boiling water for 8 minutes per pound. Steaming is an excellent method to cook fresh fish because little or no oil is used.

5. **POACH** — Select the same kinds of fish as for steaming. Again the fish must be very fresh. Do not allow the water to boil. Cook the fish submerged in water for 5 to 10 minutes. Pour sauce over fish and serve hot. I prefer steaming to poaching because more nutrients are lost in poaching.

6. **SMOKE and BAKE** — High fat content fish is preferred for smoking and baking. There are two basic ways to smoke a fish. One method is to use tea leaves and sugar. You can smoke the fish in the oven or in the wok. Another method provides similar results, but the fish is actually marinated and then deep-fried.

7. **STEW** — Large fish heads and tails are often cooked in clay pots with large amounts of water and simmered for an hour. Vegetables are added to enhance the flavor and texture of the soup.

清蒸魚

STEAMED TROUT WITH GINGER SAUCE

You must use the freshest fish for this dish because the sauce is extremely light and delicate. Steam fish the same day you purchase it.

Serves 3-4   **Difficulty level 1**

1-1 1/2	lb fresh trout*		1	tsp shredded green onion
2	tsp soy sauce		1	tsp shredded ginger
1	tsp dry sherry		1	thin slice ham, shredded
1/2	tsp salt			

1. Scale, gut, and thoroughly wash fish with cold water. Pat dry with paper towels. Make 3-4 diagonal slits across both sides of fish. Put fish in a round, heat-proof serving platter that can be fitted into a steamer or wok. If fish is too big, cut in half.

2. Sprinkle fish with soy sauce, dry sherry, and salt; spread green onion, ginger, and ham on top.

3. With protective gloves, set platter of fish on a rack in wok or steamer over 1½"-2" of boiling water. Cover and steam fish over high heat for 10-15 minutes or until firm to touch. Serve immediately.

* Sea bass or flounder may be substituted for trout.

油炸魚

DEEP-FRIED FLOUNDER

The bones of this fish are so crunchy and good, they can be eaten too! Fish bones are loaded with calcium.

Serves 4   **Difficulty level 1**

1 2/3	lb whole fish (flounder or sole)	1 1/2 TBS chopped green onion
1	TBS dry sherry	**SEASONING SAUCE:**
1/2	tsp salt	1 1/2 TBS dry sherry
1/4	cup cornstarch	1 1/2 TBS chicken stock
3-4	cups salad oil	3/4 TBS soy sauce

1. Scale, gut, and thoroughly wash fish with cold water. Pat dry with paper towels. Make deep slits at ½" intervals on thick part of body on both sides of the fish. Marinate with dry sherry and salt for 20 minutes. Pat dry with paper towels before deep-frying. Dredge lightly with cornstarch.

2. Mix seasoning sauce in a small bowl and set aside.

3. Heat wok over high heat. Add oil and heat to 375°F. Gently slide fish into hot oil and fry for 5-8 minutes or until golden brown and crispy. Drain on paper towels; place on a serving plate. Drain oil from wok.

4. Reheat 1 TBS of drained oil in the same wok. Stir-fry green onion until fragrant. Add seasoning sauce and bring to a boil; drizzle sauce over fish. Serve immediately.

糖醋魚片

FISH FILLETS WITH TOMATO SAUCE

Fish fillets cooked in this sweet and sour sauce taste like chicken. You may substitute shrimp instead of fish for this dish.

Serves 4-5   **Difficulty level 1**

1	lb white fish fillets (cod, sea bass, Pacific snapper)	**SEASONING SAUCE:**
1	egg white	1/2 cup water
1	TBS cornstarch	1/2 cup ketchup
1/2	tsp salt	1/3 cup sugar
3	cups salad oil	1/3 cup cider vinegar
1/2	cup cornstarch	1 1/2 TBS dry sherry
1/2	cup diced onion	1 TBS cornstarch
1/2	cup diced bamboo shoots*	1/2 TBS sesame oil
1/2	cup frozen green peas, thawed	1 tsp salt

1. Cut fish into 2" x 1½" x ¼" pieces. In a bowl, marinate with egg white, cornstarch, and salt about half an hour at room temperature.

2. Mix seasoning sauce in a large measuring cup and set aside.

3. Heat oil to 375°F over high heat in a large wok. Coat fish lightly in cornstarch. Fry a few pieces of fish at a time until firm, about 1 minute. Drain on paper towels. Drain oil from wok.

4. Reheat 2 TBS of drained oil in same wok. Stir-fry onion and bamboo shoots over medium-high heat. Add seasoning sauce, stirring briskly until thickened. Add green peas and fried fish. Turn off heat and stir until blended. Serve immediately.

* Parboiled carrots may be substituted for bamboo shoots.

椒鹽炸魚片

CRISPY FISH SLICES WITH SWEET AND SOUR SAUCE

My sister taught me this light batter recipe. The secret is in the water chestnut starch, which gives the crispiness. This batter is also delicious on shrimp, sliced eggplant, and zucchini.

Serves 4   **Difficulty level 1**

1	lb white fish fillets (cod, sea bass, Pacific snapper)
1/2	tsp salt
6	TBS flour
1 1/2	TBS water chestnut starch
1 1/2	TBS baking powder
3/4	cup cold water
3	cups salad oil

1	tsp chopped garlic
1	tsp chopped green onion

SWEET AND SOUR SAUCE:

1/4	cup water
2	TBS sugar
2	TBS ketchup
2	TBS cider vinegar
1	tsp sesame oil

1. Cut fish into 2" x 1½" x 1/4" pieces. In a bowl, marinate fish with salt for 20 minutes at room temperature.

2. Stir flour, chestnut starch, and baking powder with water in another bowl. Stir until batter resembles pancake batter. Let rest for 15 minutes.

3. Mix sauce ingredients in a measuring cup and set aside.

4. Heat oil to 375°F over high heat in a large wok. Coat fish with flour batter. Fry, a few pieces at a time, about 3 minutes until golden brown and crispy. Drain on paper towels.

5. Heat 1 TBS oil over medium-high heat in a small saucepan. Stir-fry garlic until fragrant. Add sweet and sour sauce. Bring to a boil. Sprinkle with chopped green onion. Pour sauce into a small bowl. Serve sauce as a dip with fish.

青椒蒸魚

STEAMED FISH STEAKS WITH PEPPERS

This is a colorful and healthy way to serve fish. There is very little oil in this recipe and the vegetables are full of vitamins.

Serves 5-6   **Difficulty level 1**

1 1/2	lb fresh fish steaks (salmon, mahi mahi, trout)
1	TBS dry sherry
1/2	tsp salt
1/2	red pepper, shredded
1/2	green pepper, shredded
1/4	cup shredded bamboo shoots
2	TBS shredded green onion
1	TBS shredded ginger

SEASONING SAUCE:

1 1/2	TBS fermented black beans
1	TBS chopped dry red pepper
2	TBS soy sauce
1	TBS salad oil
1	tsp minced garlic
1	tsp sesame oil

1. Wash fish under cold water and pat dry with paper towels. Place fish with skin side up on a large, heat-proof serving platter. Sprinkle with dry sherry and salt. Place all shredded vegetables on top of fish.

2. Soak black beans in a small bowl in cold water for 5 minutes. Rinse and drain well. Mince. Cut away tips of the dry pepper. Chop and remove all seeds. Mix black beans and dry pepper in a small bowl with all remaining ingredients in seasoning sauce. Pour sauce over fish and vegetables.

3. With protective gloves, set platter on a rack in steamer or wok over 1½"-2" of boiling water. Cover and steam fish over high heat for 10-12 minutes, or until firm to touch. Serve immediately.

SMOKED AND BAKED FISH STEAKS

Smoking fish in the oven is a simplified modern method for cooking this traditional dish. Smoke will come out of the oven while baking, so open some windows. Or, you may smoke outdoors in a domed smoker. If you prefer to bake the fish instead, eliminate the tea and sugar in this recipe. This dish makes an excellent cold appetizer for a formal dinner and is also perfect for picnics. Smoked fish steaks will keep in the refrigerator for several days.

Serves 3-4   **Difficulty level 1**

1	lb fish steaks or fillets	1/2 cup black tea leaves
	(salmon, red snapper, or mackerel)	2 TBS sugar
4	TBS soy sauce	1 tsp sesame oil
1	TBS sugar	
1	TBS dry sherry	
1	tsp salt	
4	green onions, cut 2" lengths	
4	slices ginger, smashed	

1. Spray top rack of oven with vegetable cooking oil. Preheat oven to 500°F.

2. Cut fish into 3" x 1½" x 1" pieces. Marinate fish with next 6 ingredients in a bowl for at least 20 minutes at room temperature.

3. Sprinkle tea and sugar in a large pan lined with foil and place pan on the bottom oven rack. Put fish, skin side up, on the greased top rack. Bake for 10-15 minutes or until fish flakes easily with a fork. Remove and brush with sesame oil.* Serve hot or cold.

* Parsley, cilantro or lemon slices may be used for garnish.

豆豉魚片

FISH FILLETS WITH FERMENTED BLACK BEANS

The flavorful combination of black beans, garlic, ginger, and peppers makes this dish tasty and aromatic.

Serves 4   **Difficulty level 2**

1	lb firm, white fish fillet (sea bass, yellow pike, cod)	
2	tsp dry sherry	
1/2	tsp salt	
1/4	tsp white pepper	
1/2	TBS fermented black beans	
2-3	cups salad oil	
1/2	TBS chopped garlic	
1/2	TBS chopped ginger	
2	TBS chopped green onion	
1	TBS chopped dried red pepper (optional)	

SEASONING SAUCE:

3	TBS chicken stock
1	tsp cornstarch
1	tsp dry sherry
1/2	tsp salt
1/2	tsp sesame oil
1/4	tsp white pepper

1. Score top side of fish fillet lengthwise and crosswise at ¼" intervals and ⅛" deep. Cut into 1"-2" squares. Marinate with dry sherry, salt, and pepper for about half an hour at room temperature.

2. Soak black beans in a small bowl in cold water for 5 minutes. Rinse and drain well. Chop into small pieces.

3. Mix seasoning sauce in a small bowl and set aside.

4. Heat wok over high heat. Add oil and heat to 375°F. Fry all fish pieces quickly, <u>without stirring</u>, about 10 seconds over medium-high heat. In colander, over a bowl, drain fish.

5. Reheat 2 TBS of drained oil in same wok. Stir-fry beans, garlic, and ginger for 10 seconds. Add seasoning sauce and fish, and continue to stir gently. Add green onion and red pepper. Mix well and serve immediately.

FISH FILLETS WITH OYSTER SAUCE

This dish is simple to make and delicious. Even children will like it. One trick when cooking this recipe—make sure the wok is hot before adding oil. This prevents the fish from sticking.

Serves 4   **Difficulty level 2**

1	lb firm, white fish fillets (cod, sea bass, Pacific snapper)	
1	TBS cornstarch	
1	egg white	
1/2	TBS dry sherry	
1/2	tsp salt	
2-3	cups salad oil	
1	green onion, chopped	
5	slices peeled ginger	
1	clove garlic, chopped	
1/2	carrot, parboiled & sliced	

SEASONING SAUCE:

1/2	cup water
4 1/2	TBS oyster sauce
1/2	TBS sugar
1/2	TBS cornstarch
1/2	TBS sesame oil

1. Cut fish into 2" x 1" x ¼" pieces. In a bowl, marinate fish with cornstarch, egg white, dry sherry, and salt for half an hour at room temperature.

2. Mix seasoning sauce in a measuring cup and set aside.

3. Heat wok over high heat. Add oil and heat to 400°F. Add 2 TBS cold oil to the fish to prevent it from sticking together; mix thoroughly. Fry fish over high heat for 20 seconds, <u>without</u> <u>stirring</u>. In colander, over a bowl, drain fish.

4. Reheat 2 TBS of drained oil in same wok. Stir-fry green onion, ginger, and garlic over medium-high heat until fragrant. Add carrot and fish. Pour in the seasoning sauce. Stir carefully and serve immediately.

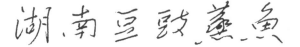

STEAMED FISH WITH FERMENTED BLACK BEANS, HUNANESE STYLE

You can assemble all ingredients an hour ahead and store in the refrigerator until ready to steam.

Serves 4   **Difficulty level 2**

1 1/2	lb whole fish (sea bass, carp, trout, etc.)*	1	TBS dry sherry
1	tsp salt	1	TBS soy sauce
1	TBS fermented black beans	1	TBS chopped green onion
1	TBS chopped dried red pepper	1	TBS salad oil
1	TBS chopped ginger	1/2	tsp sugar
1	TBS chopped ham		

1. Scale, gut, and thoroughly wash fish with cold water. Pat dry with paper towels. Make diagonal slits 1/4" deep at 1/2" intervals on both sides of the fish. Sprinkle fish, inside and out, with salt.

2. Soak black beans in a small bowl in cold water for 5 minutes. Rinse and drain well. Cut away tips of dried pepper. Chop and remove all seeds. Mix beans and red pepper with the remaining ingredients in a bowl.

3. Place fish on a platter with the back facing up. Pour sauce over fish.

4. With protective gloves, set platter on a rack in wok or steamer over 1½"-2" of boiling water. Cover and steam fish over high heat for about 10 minutes or until firm to touch. Serve immediately.

* You may steam two 3/4 lb fish, such as trout, on the same platter for 8 minutes.

红烧鱼

BRAISED SOY SAUCE FISH, SHANGHAI STYLE

My mother often served this fish at home because it is good, hot or cold. When the fish is served cold, the sauce resembles an aspic.

Serves 4   **Difficulty level 3**

1 1/2 lb whole fish (sea bass, carp, perch, scup, etc.)	**SEASONING SAUCE:**
1/2 tsp salt	3/4 cup water
1/2 cup salad oil	5 TBS soy sauce
2 slices ginger	2 TBS light brown sugar
1 bunch green onions, cut in half	1 TBS dry sherry
1/3 cup sliced bamboo shoots	
1/3 cup black mushrooms, softened and sliced	

1. Scale, gut, and thoroughly wash fish with cold water. Pat dry with paper towels. Make 3-4 diagonal slits across both sides of the fish.* Sprinkle fish, inside and out, with salt. Let stand for 10 minutes at room temperature.

2. Mix seasoning sauce in a measuring cup and set aside.

3. Heat wok over high heat. Add oil and heat to 375°F. Add ginger slices. Gently add fish and fry over medium-high heat for about 3-4 minutes on each side. Oil will splatter. Turn fish carefully. Add green onions, bamboo shoots, and mushrooms. When fish is golden brown, pour off excess oil. Add seasoning sauce; cover and bring to a boil. Reduce heat to low and cook slowly, covered, for 3 minutes. Remove cover; increase heat, and baste fish until a little more than ½ cup liquid remains. Serve hot or cold.

* Cut fish in half if it is too big. After cooking, reassemble the fish by placing the two halves on the plate as a whole fish. Arrange green onions, bamboo shoots, and mushrooms to cover the division.

糖醋松鼠魚

SQUIRREL FISH WITH SWEET AND SOUR SAUCE

This dish is often served at banquets. The fish head looks like a squirrel, hence the name. The sweet and sour sauce is exceptionally good.

Serves 4-6   **Difficulty level 3**

2	dried black mushrooms	**SWEET & SOUR SAUCE:**	
1/4	cup peas, shelled	1/2	cup sugar
1	small carrot	1/2	cup white vinegar
1	whole sea bass or	1/2	cup mushroom stock
	red snapper (2 lb)	1/4	cup ketchup
3	cups salad oil	2	tsp salt
1/2	cup flour	2	tsp dry sherry
1	small onion, diced	2	tsp soy sauce
4	water chestnuts, diced		
1	tsp minced garlic		
1 1/2	TBS cornstarch mixed with 2 TBS water		

1. Soak mushrooms in ½ cup warm water in a small bowl for 15 minutes. Save liquid for seasoning sauce. Cut off mushroom stems and discard. Dice mushrooms.

2. Parboil peas and carrots in 6 cups of boiling water for a few minutes or until tender. Drain and rinse with cold water. Dice carrots.

3. Scale, gut, and thoroughly wash fish with cold water. Pat dry with paper towels. Remove head at the point where it joins the body.* Turn head upside down, using a·few sharp blows with a cleaver, break head bone in the middle. With the palm of the hand, press down firmly on top of the head to flatten. Lay fish on its side and split in half, cutting along the backbone but not through tail. Lift backbone out, severing it at the base of the tail. Score flesh side of each fillet with crisscrossing diagonal cuts 1" apart and almost down to the skin. Fish should be joined at the tail.

4. Mix seasoning sauce in a bowl and set aside.

5. Heat wok over high heat. Add oil and heat to 375°F. Sprinkle flour on a piece of waxed paper and press scored sides of fish into flour. Next, coat the skin side. Hold fish by the tail, shake off excess flour and gently place in hot oil. Flour the head and add it to oil in wok. Fry for 5-8 minutes until golden brown. Drain on paper towels. Place fish, skin side down, on a heated platter and set head back in its original position. Drain oil from wok.

6. Reheat 2 TBS of drained oil in same wok. Add mushrooms, peas, carrots, onion, water chestnuts, and garlic, and stir for 3 minutes. Add seasoning sauce and bring to a boil. Stir in cornstarch mixture and cook until vegetables are glazed. Pour over fish and serve immediately.

If you do not wish to serve the fish head, save it for fish stock.

廣式清燉魚

STEAMED FLOUNDER, CANTONESE STYLE

This is the most famous Cantonese method of preparing steamed fish. The sauce is cooked separately and poured onto the juicy and tender fish.

Serves 4   **Difficulty level 3**

1	whole flounder, sole, or whitefish (1 2/3 lb)*
1	TBS dry sherry
1	tsp salt
1/2	cup shredded green onion
3	TBS shredded ginger
3	TBS cilantro
dash of pepper	
3	TBS salad oil

SEASONING SAUCE:

1/2	cup chicken stock
1	TBS soy sauce
1	tsp sesame oil
1/4	tsp salt
1	tsp cornstarch mixed with 1 TBS water

1. Scale, gut, and thoroughly wash fish. Pat dry with paper towels. Make diagonal slits at 3/4" intervals across both sides of fish. On a round, heat-proof plate, marinate fish with dry sherry, salt, half the green onion, and half the ginger for 20 minutes at room temperature.

2. With protective gloves, set platter on a rack in wok or steamer over 1½"-2" of boiling water. Cover and steam fish over high heat for 12 minutes, or until firm to touch. Remove fish and discard the liquid and green onions. Sprinkle fish with remaining green onions, ginger, cilantro, and pepper. Heat 3 TBS oil to boiling in small pan. Drizzle boiling oil over vegetables and fish.

3. In a small saucepan, bring stock, soy sauce, sesame oil, and salt to a boil. Stir in cornstarch mixture and cook until thickened. Pour sauce over fish. Serve immediately.

* Other kinds of fresh fish such as rockfish, kingfish and carp may also be used for steaming.

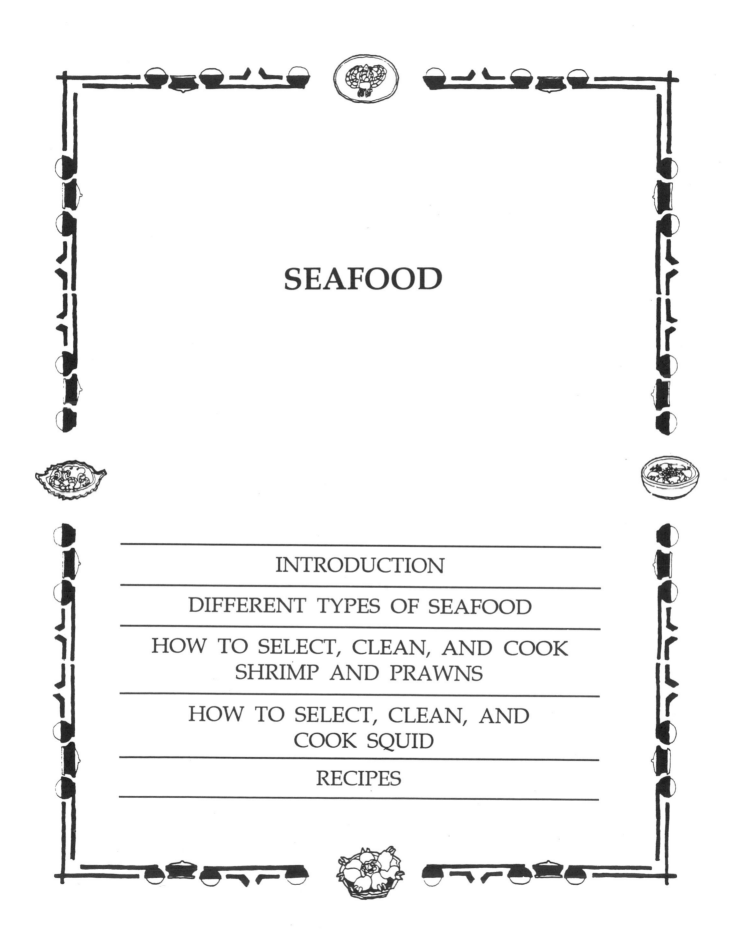

SEAFOOD

SEAFOOD

INTRODUCTION

Chinese love to eat all kinds of seafood, the most common being shrimp and prawns. For this chapter, I have selected some of my family's favorite recipes. They are easy to prepare, and the ingredients are available all year around in any supermarket.

DIFFERENT TYPES OF SEAFOOD

Since prawns and shrimp are similar in all respects except for size, they are both called "Hsia" in China. Prawns are more expensive and are often served in banquets. Shrimp is very versatile and can be cooked with various foods.

Crabs are popular in China too. I remember when I was growing up in Shanghai, we used to eat fresh water crabs by the dozens. My mother would steam live crabs with ginger and green onions and serve them on a table covered with newspaper or plastic cloth. Each of us would eat several crabs at one sitting. Chinese crabs are not as large as the ones in San Francisco, but they are exceptionally flavorful.

Lobsters are rather rare in China, except around the Canton area. They are often cooked the same way as large sea water crabs. Raw oysters are rarely eaten in China because of contamination. When they are served, they are frequently coated with a batter and deep-fried. Because fresh oysters do not travel well, they are usually sold in cans.

Abalone in its fresh form is often imported into China from other countries. The canned ones come from Australia and Mexico. Abalone is expensive and difficult to prepare. It is most important not to overcook abalone because the texture becomes tough and chewy. Excellent abalone soup can be made from the liquid in the can.

Clams and scallops are cooked many different ways in China. When buying them, the shells should be tightly closed. The ones that are open are usually dead and no longer edible. Already shelled ones must be kept on ice. Squid and cuttlefish are less common in China. Since they die as soon as they are out of the sea, their freshness depends on how soon they reach the markets.

HOW TO SELECT, CLEAN, AND COOK SHRIMP AND PRAWNS

Select shrimp and prawns that have a bluish-grey color. They are better for stir-frying. Their flesh should be firm and resilient. Unfortunately, many of the shrimp sold in the United States come already frozen. Therefore, it is hard to judge freshness. Do not refreeze thawed shrimp. They should be used as soon as possible.

To clean shrimp, follow these easy steps:

1.   Peel off the first 3 sections of the shell with the thumb.

2.   Pull off the tail section while squeezing it gently.

3.   Butterfly shrimp: With a small paring knife, cut shrimp three-fourths of the way through along center back.

4.   Remove the black vein with the tip of the knife. Turn shrimp to the underside and remove the bluish vein.

4 STEPS TO SHELL AND CLEAN SHRIMP

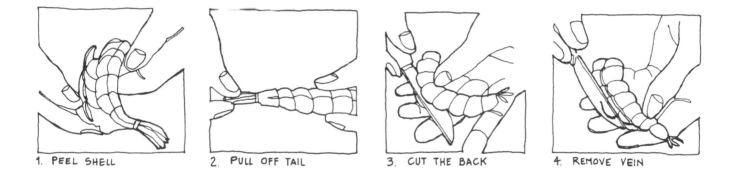

1. PEEL SHELL   2. PULL OFF TAIL   3. CUT THE BACK   4. REMOVE VEIN

There are many methods to cook shrimp and prawns. Choose prawns or jumbo shrimp that are 4"-6" long for braising, stewing, and deep-frying. Large and medium-sized shrimp are perfect for stir-frying. Small shrimp, that are cheaper and take longer to shell and clean, are used more often to make into shrimp balls or pastes. Since shrimp is so lean, many recipes add minced pork or other ingredients to enhance the flavor and texture.

HOW TO SELECT, CLEAN, AND COOK SQUID

Squid deteriorates quickly. It is important to cook it as soon as possible. Fresh squid is firm and smooth with the skin wrapped tightly around the body. The flesh should spring back when poked with a finger.

To clean squid use the following steps:

1. Open the underside of the body with a sharp knife or scissors.

2. Remove and discard the long, transparent, sword-shaped shell, and all the material that comes off easily from the body.

3. Peel away the pink membrane from the hood with your fingers and discard. Rinse the squid with cold water.

4. Cut the squid lengthwise into 1"-1½" strips.

5. Score squid by making diagonal cuts 2/3 deep, using an angled cut about ⅛" apart.

6. Turn the squid and score again to form diamond shaped cuts.

6 STEPS TO CLEAN SQUID

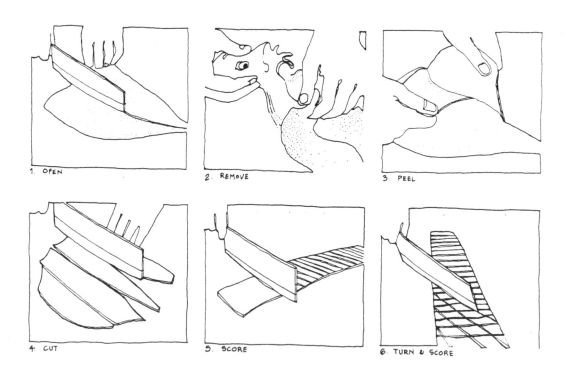

1. OPEN   2. REMOVE   3. PEEL

4. CUT   5. SCORE   6. TURN & SCORE

Squid must not be overcooked, otherwise it will be tough and chewy. There are two basic methods of cooking squid before stir-frying with other ingredients:

1. **Parboiling** — Plunge squid into a large pot with 6 cups of boiling water. The minute squid curls and turns white, remove with a strainer. Rinse with cold water and drain well.

2. **Pan-frying** — Use ½-1 cup of warm oil to seal in the juiciness and the crispness of squid. The minute it curls, remove and drain well.

大蒜炸蝦

CRISPY SHRIMP WITH GARLIC

The shrimp in this dish is finger licking good. Leaving the shells on make the insides juicy and tender and the outside crispy. The best way to eat crispy shrimp is with chopsticks or fingers.

Serves 4-5   **Difficulty level 1**

1	lb raw, medium-sized shrimp	1	tsp salt
1/4	tsp ginger juice	2	TBS chopped garlic
1	TBS cornstarch	1/2	TBS chopped dried red pepper
1	TBS dry sherry		
3	cups salad oil	1	TBS minced green onion

1. Rinse shrimp and drain well. Do not remove shell. With scissors, cut off legs and open their backs. With knife, devein shrimp by making a cut down the back about ¼" deep. Lift out black vein with tip of knife.

2. Make ginger juice by pressing pieces of fresh ginger through a garlic press. Mix shrimp with ginger juice, cornstarch, and sherry in a bowl. Marinate for 20 minutes at room temperature.

3. Heat oil to 375°F over high heat in a large wok. Fry shrimp for 1-1½ minutes until shrimp turns pink and crispy. Remove shrimp with a strainer, and drain on paper towels. Drain oil from wok.

4. Reheat same wok without oil over medium heat. Add salt, stir in garlic and dried red pepper, and cook until fragrant. Return shrimp to wok; toss to mix well. Garnish with green onion and serve hot.

青豆蝦仁

SHRIMP WITH GREEN PEAS

Sealing shrimp in oil before stir-frying with vegetables is a technique used by most restaurants. The result is succulent shrimp.

Serves 4　　　　　　　　　　　　　　　　　　　　　　**Difficulty level 1**

1	lb raw, large-sized shrimp	1/2-1	cup salad oil
4-5	drops ginger juice	1/2	tsp salt
1	tsp salt	1	cup green peas*, parboiled
1	tsp cornstarch		or frozen (defrosted)
1	tsp dry sherry	1	tsp cornstarch mixed
1	green onion, cut 2" lengths		with 2 TBS water

1. Wash, drain, and shell shrimp. With knife, butterfly and devein shrimp. Make ginger juice by pressing pieces of fresh ginger through a garlic press. Mix shrimp with ginger juice, salt, cornstarch, sherry, and green onions in a bowl.

2. Heat wok over high heat; add oil. When oil is warm (320°F), add shrimp mixture. Stir until shrimp just begin to turn pink, about 30 seconds. In colander, over a bowl, drain shrimp. Discard green onions.

3. Reheat 2 TBS of drained oil in the same wok over medium heat. Add ½ tsp salt and green peas. Stir for 1 minute until peas are heated. Stir in cornstarch mixture. Add shrimp. Stir briefly and serve immediately.

* 1/4 lb snow peas may be substituted for green peas. Stir-fry 2-3 minutes until tender crisp. 1/4 cup each of diced ham, water chestnuts, and bamboo shoots may be added with the peas. Reduce the amount of peas from 1 cup to 1/2 cup.

SWEET AND SOUR SHRIMP

You may wish to double the sauce because it is so good. Serve on rice to fully enjoy extra sauce.

Serves 4-5   **Difficulty level 1**

1	lb raw, large-sized shrimp	**SWEET AND SOUR SAUCE:**	
1	egg white	1/3	cup ketchup
1	TBS cornstarch	1/3	cup water
1/2	tsp salt	3	TBS sugar
2-3	cups salad oil	3	TBS cider vinegar
1/3	cup cornstarch	1	TBS dry sherry
1/2	cup diced onion	2	tsp cornstarch
1/3	cup diced mushrooms	1	tsp salt
1/3	cup cooked green peas	1	tsp sesame oil

1. Wash, drain, and shell shrimp. With knife, butterfly and devein shrimp. Mix shrimp with egg white, 1 TBS cornstarch, and salt in a bowl. Marinate for half an hour at room temperature.

2. Mix sweet and sour sauce in a bowl and set aside.

3. Heat oil to 375°F over high heat in a large wok. Coat shrimp in 1/3 cup cornstarch, and fry for 1 minute or until color changes. Remove shrimp and drain well on paper towels. Drain oil from wok.

4. Reheat 2 TBS of drained oil in the same wok over medium heat. Stir-fry onion and mushrooms. Add sweet and sour sauce. Stir briskly until thickened. Add green peas and shrimp, stirring until blended. Serve immediately.

SHRIMP WITH LOBSTER SAUCE

My students are always surprised to discover that this dish does not contain lobster. It is so named because the sauce is used to cook the famous Cantonese lobster dish.

Serves 4   **Difficulty level 1**

1	lb raw, large-sized shrimp
2	tsp dry sherry
1/2	TBS cornstarch
1 1/2	TBS fermented black beans
4	TBS salad oil
2	slices ginger
2	cloves garlic, crushed
1/4	lb ground pork or beef
1 1/2	TBS cornstarch mixed with 1/4 cup water
1	egg, beaten

SEASONING SAUCE:

1	cup water
1	TBS soy sauce
1/2	tsp salt
1/2	tsp sesame oil
1/4	tsp sugar
dash of pepper	

1. Wash, drain, and shell shrimp. With knife, butterfly and devein shrimp. Mix shrimp with sherry and cornstarch in a bowl.

2. Soak beans in cold water in a small bowl for 5 minutes. Rinse, drain, and mince.

3. Mix seasoning sauce in a large measuring cup and set aside.

4. Heat wok over high heat; add oil. When oil is warm (320°F), add shrimp mixture. Stir until shrimp just begin to turn pink, about 30 seconds. Remove shrimp and leave as much oil as you can in wok.

5. Reheat wok over medium-high heat. Add ginger, garlic, and black beans; stir. Add meat; stir-fry until cooked. Stir in seasoning sauce mixture, and bring to a boil. Cover and simmer for 2 minutes. Remove garlic and ginger. Stir in cornstarch mixture and shrimp. Add beaten egg; stir once or twice. Serve hot.

腰果蝦仁

STIR-FRIED SHRIMP WITH CASHEWS

For those who enjoy spicy and pungent food, this shrimp dish cooked with dried red pepper is a must.

Serves 4-5   **Difficulty level 1**

1	lb raw, large-sized shrimp	**SEASONING SAUCE:**	
1	TBS cornstarch	1 1/2	TBS water
1	TBS dry sherry	1 1/2	TBS soy sauce
1	TBS egg white	2	tsp sugar
1/2	tsp salt	1/2	TBS dry sherry
1/2-1	cup salad oil	1	tsp cornstarch
1/2	TBS chopped, dried red peppers	1	tsp cider vinegar
1	green onion, cut 1" length		
1	green pepper, cut 1/2" cubes		
1/2	cup unsalted, roasted cashews or peanuts		

1. Wash, drain, and shell shrimp. With knife, butterfly and devein shrimp. Mix shrimp with cornstarch, sherry, egg white, and salt in a bowl.

2. Mix seasoning sauce in a small bowl and set aside.

3. Heat wok over high heat; add oil. When oil is warm (320°F), add shrimp mixture. Stir until shrimp just begin to turn pink, about 30 seconds. In colander, over a bowl, drain shrimp.

4. Reheat 2 TBS of drained oil in same wok over medium-high heat. Stir-fry dried peppers and green onion until fragrant. Add green peppers; stir lightly. Add shrimp and seasoning sauce; stir quickly until well mixed. Remove from heat and mix in nuts. Serve immediately.

蝦仁鮮貝

SHRIMP AND SCALLOPS WITH CASHEW NUTS

This is a typical Cantonese seafood dish. Cashew nuts must be added at the end with the heat turned off, otherwise the nuts will lose their crispness.

Serves 4-5   **Difficulty level 1**

1/2	lb raw, large-sized shrimp	**SEASONING SAUCE:**	
1/2	lb fresh scallops	1/2	cup chicken stock
1/2	egg white	1	TBS soy sauce
1	TBS dry sherry	1/2	TBS cornstarch
2	tsp cornstarch	1	tsp sesame oil
1/2	tsp salt	1/4	tsp salt
1/2	tsp sugar	dash of pepper	
2	stalks celery		
1	carrot	1/2-1	cup salad oil
2	green onions	1/2	cup unsalted, roasted
6	oz fresh mushrooms		cashew nuts

1. Wash, drain, and shell shrimp. With knife, butterfly and devein shrimp. Place in a bowl. Cut scallops into 1½" x ½" pieces. Add to bowl with shrimp. Mix seafood with egg white, dry sherry, cornstarch, salt, and sugar. Marinate for 15 minutes at room temperature.

2. Peel celery and carrot. Cut into thin diagonal slices. Cut green onions into ½" pieces. Slice mushrooms.

3. Mix seasoning sauce in a measuring cup and set aside.

4. Heat wok over high heat; add oil. When oil is warm (320°F), add shrimp and scallops mixture. Stir until shrimp just begin to turn pink, about 30 seconds. In colander, over a bowl, drain seafood.

5. Reheat 2 TBS of drained oil in same wok over medium-high heat. Add vegetables and stir for 1 minute. Stir in seasoning sauce. Add seafood and cook for 30 seconds. Remove from heat and stir in nuts. Serve immediately.

BUTTERFLY SHRIMP WITH SNOW PEAS AND STRAW MUSHROOMS

The smooth texture of straw mushrooms in contrast to the crunchy snow peas makes this dish a big hit.

Serves 4-5   **Difficulty level 2**

1	lb raw, large-sized shrimp
4-5	drops ginger juice
1	tsp cornstarch
1	tsp dry sherry
1/2	tsp salt
1	green onion, cut 2" lengths
1/2	lb snow peas
8	large fresh or canned water chestnuts
1/2	cup unpeeled straw mushrooms*
1/2-1	cup salad oil

SEASONING SAUCE:

1/2	cup chicken stock
2	tsp soy sauce
1	tsp salt
pinch of sugar	
1	large clove garlic, minced
2	tsp shredded ginger
1	tsp cornstarch mixed with 2 TBS water

1. Wash, drain, and shell shrimp. With knife, butterfly and devein shrimp. Make ginger juice by pressing chopped pieces of fresh ginger through a garlic press. Mix shrimp with ginger juice, cornstarch, dry sherry, salt, and green onion in a bowl.

2. Snap off both ends of snow peas and remove strings from the sides. Wash and drain well. Peel and rinse water chestnuts. Slice thinly, crosswise. Drain straw mushrooms.

3. Mix seasoning sauce in a measuring cup and set aside.

4. Heat wok over high heat; add oil. When oil is warm (320°F), add shrimp mixture. Stir until shrimp just begin to turn pink, about 30 seconds. In colander, over a bowl, drain shrimp.

5. Reheat 2 TBS of drained oil in same wok over medium-high heat. Stir-fry mushrooms for 30 seconds. Add garlic and ginger; stir-fry another 30 seconds. Add snow peas and water chestnuts, stirring briskly for 1

minute. Add seasoning sauce and bring to a boil, continuing to stir-fry until snow peas are bright green. Push ingredients out of liquid; dribble cornstarch mixture into liquid, stirring until slightly thickened. Add shrimp; stir all ingredients together briefly. Serve immediately.

* Fresh or canned mushrooms may be substituted for straw mushrooms.

BAKED SEAFOOD IN SWAN-SHAPED FOIL PACKETS

I featured this dish in a cooking lesson on CNN-TV because it is so healthy, and the presentation is surprisingly dramatic and beautiful. The Swans can be wrapped an hour ahead, and then baked just before serving. There is no mess to clean up either.

Serves 6   **Difficulty level 2**

2/3	lb raw, large-sized shrimp
2/3	lb raw scallops
1	TBS dry sherry
1/2	tsp salt
1/4	tsp white pepper
1/4	lb spinach
12	slices bamboo shoots
12	slices carrots
12	button mushrooms
cilantro for garnish	

SEASONING SAUCE:

2	TBS chicken stock
1 1/2	TBS soy sauce
1	TBS dry sherry
1/2	TBS chopped garlic
1/2	TBS chopped green onion
1/2	TBS chili oil (optional)
1/2	tsp salt
1/2	tsp sugar
1/2	tsp sesame oil

1. Wash, drain, and shell shrimp. With knife, butterfly and devein shrimp. Rinse scallops with cold water; drain well on paper towels. Mix seafood with dry sherry, salt, and pepper in a bowl. Marinate for 10 minutes at room temperature.

2. Mix seasoning sauce in a bowl and set aside.

3. Preheat oven to 500°F. To prepare each swan packet: Tear off six 12" x 12" sheets of aluminum foil. For each packet, place 1/6 of spinach leaves in the middle of the foil. Add 2 slices each bamboo shoots and carrots,

and 2 mushrooms. Top with ⅙ of scallops and shrimp mixture.* Add 1 TBS seasoning sauce and a sprig of cilantro (fig. 1). Bring corners B & D together; fold over several times to form body. Twist corner C gently to form a small tail. Shape corner A into a long neck and bend the end forward to form a small head, forming a swan-like shape (fig. 2). Place packets in pan. Bake for 10-15 minutes or until done.

4. To serve, arrange packets on a large platter. Garnish with cilantro.

Fish fillets and oysters may be substituted for shrimp and scallops. Other vegetables such as zucchini, celery, and Chinese black mushrooms may also be used.

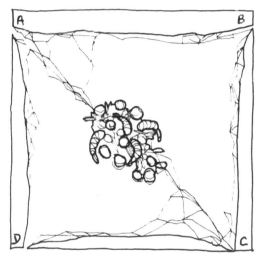

1. FOLD

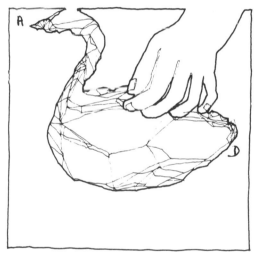

2. WRAP

蒸明蝦

STEAMED FLOWER-SHAPED PRAWNS WITH CHINESE GREEN CABBAGE

This is a delicious and colorful dish that is great for special occasions or holidays.

Serves 4-5   **Difficulty level 3**

12	prawns or	2	TBS finely chopped
	1 lb raw, jumbo shrimp		onion
1/2	TBS dry sherry	1	tsp minced ginger
1	tsp salt	**SEASONING SAUCE:**	
1	lb Chinese green cabbage*	1/2	cup chicken stock
3	TBS salad oil	2	TBS ketchup
1/2	cup chicken stock	1	TBS soy sauce
1/2	tsp salt	1/2	tsp cornstarch
3	slices ginger, shredded	1/4	tsp sugar
2	green onions, cut 2" lengths	1/4	tsp sesame oil

1. Wash, drain, and shell prawns, leaving the tail shells attached. With knife, butterfly and devein prawns. Make a small slit in the middle of the body (fig. 1). Pull tail through the slit (fig. 2). Mix prawns with dry sherry and 1 tsp salt in a bowl and marinate for about 5 minutes at room temperature.

2. Wash and drain green cabbage. Parboil in a large pot of 6 cups of boiling water for about 1-2 minutes until softened. Rinse with cold water and drain well. Cut lengthwise in half.

3. Heat 2 TBS oil in skillet over medium heat. Stir-fry cabbage for 30 seconds. Add ½ cup stock and ½ tsp salt; cook 2 minutes, covered. In colander, drain cabbage.

4. Set prawns, tails up, on a heat-proof, round platter (fig. 3). Place ginger slices and green onions on top. Set platter on a rack in wok or steamer over 1½"-2" of boiling water. Cover and steam over high heat for 5-10 minutes until cooked. Discard ginger and green onions; drain liquid from plate.

5. While shrimp is steaming, mix seasoning sauce in a measuring cup and set aside.

6. Heat remaining 1 TBS oil in a small pan over medium heat. Add onion and minced ginger. Cook, stirring, until onion becomes soft and slightly brown. Add seasoning sauce; bring to a boil. This sauce may be prepared in advance and reheated just before serving.

7. To serve, arrange cabbage around steamed prawns. Pour seasoning sauce over prawns. Serve immediately.

Broccoli, cauliflower, or spinach may be substituted for green cabbage. If spinach is used, do not parboil before stir-frying. Simply stir-fry with oil and add salt. Drain and arrange around steamed prawns.

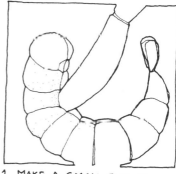

1. MAKE A SMALL SLIT IN THE MIDDLE OF THE SHRIMP

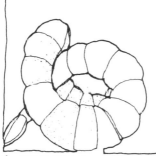

2. PUSH THE TAIL THROUGH

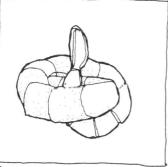

3. SET PRAWNS WITH TAIL POINTING UPWARD

海鮮盤

SEAFOOD IN A POTATO BIRD'S NEST

This scrumptious dish is served at many Chinese banquets and is definitely one of my students' favorites.

Serves 4-5   **Difficulty level 3**

1	Potato Bird's Nest (optional)
6	fresh small squid*
12	raw, large-sized shrimp
6	fresh scallops or 1/4 lb
	Bay scallops
1	TBS cornstarch
1/2	TBS dry sherry
1/2	tsp salt
1/2-1	cup salad oil
1	green onion, cut 1" length
6	slices ginger
1	cup snow peas, strings removed
1/4	cup bamboo shoots, sliced
1/2	carrot, parboiled & sliced

SEASONING SAUCE:

3	TBS water
1/2	TBS dry sherry
1	tsp sugar
1	tsp cornstarch
1	tsp sesame oil
1/2	tsp salt
1/8	tsp black pepper

green lettuce for garnish

1. Prepare Potato Bird's Nest. (See following recipe.)

2. Cut open squid with scissors, and remove all material from body. Peel off pink skin and rinse well. Score squid by making diagonal cuts to 2/3 deep on the <u>inside</u> <u>surface</u>, using an angled cut, crisscross fashion. Cut in half lengthwise. Place squid in a bowl.

3. Wash, drain, and shell shrimp. With knife, butterfly and devein shrimp. Put shrimp in same bowl with squid. Add scallops, cornstarch, dry sherry, and salt. Toss to mix well; set aside.

4. Mix seasoning sauce in a small bowl and set aside.

5. Heat wok over high heat; then add oil. When oil is warm (325°F), stir-fry seafood mixture, until shrimp just begin to turn pink and squid start to curl. Do not overcook. In colander, over a bowl, drain seafood.

6. Reheat 2 TBS of drained oil in the same wok over medium-high heat. Stir-fry green onion and ginger until fragrant. Remove ginger. Add snow peas, bamboo shoots, and carrot. Stir slightly. Add seafood and seasoning sauce; stir quickly over high heat until mixed well. Remove and place in the Bird's Nest or serve on a platter.

* ¼ lb firm white fish may be substituted for squid, or use 1 lb shrimp or scallops for seafood in this recipe.

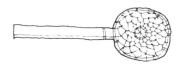

POTATO BIRD'S NEST

This potato basket may be used with many stir-fry dishes, such as Shrimp with Cashews or Shrimp with Green Peas. You can fry the potato basket ahead and store in an airtight plastic bag for a day or two. Before serving, reheat in low oven about 300°F for 5 minutes.

Makes one 10" basket   **Difficulty level 2**

2	medium-sized potatoes
1/4	cup cornstarch
6	cups salad oil

1. Rinse potatoes with cold water; peel. Shred potatoes to make about 2 cups. Place potatoes in a large bowl half- filled with cold water for about 1 hour, changing water 2-3 times to remove starch. Drain well in colander. Mix potatoes with cornstarch.

2. Spray two 10" metal strainers with vegetable cooking oil. Arrange shredded potatoes on one strainer to make a basket shape (fig. 1 on following page). Place a second strainer on top of potatoes (fig. 2).

3. Heat oil to 375°F in a 14" wok over high heat. Fry potatoes held in between 2 strainers until crisp and golden brown, about 5-10 minutes. Drain well on paper towels.

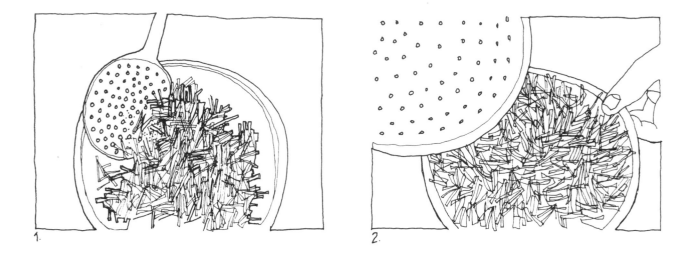

魚香魷魚、

STIR-FRIED SQUID, SZECHUAN STYLE

In Szechuan, squid is often cooked with lots of garlic, ginger, and hot bean paste. If you like spicy food, you will love this dish.

Serves 4   **Difficulty level 3**

2/3	lb fresh squid	5	water chestnuts
1	TBS cornstarch	1	cup snow peas, strings
1/2	TBS dry sherry		removed
1/3	tsp salt		
1/2	egg white	**SEASONING SAUCE:**	
1	TBS black fungus*	2 1/2	TBS water
1/2-1	cup salad oil	1 1/2	TBS oyster sauce
1	TBS chopped green onion	1/2	TBS dry sherry
1	TBS chopped ginger	1	tsp sugar
1	TBS chopped garlic	1	tsp cornstarch
1	tsp hot bean sauce (optional)	1	tsp brown vinegar

1. Cut open squid with scissors and remove all material from body. Peel off pink skin and rinse well. Score squid by making diagonal cuts to 2/3 deep on the <u>inside</u> <u>surface</u>, using an angled cut, crisscross fashion. Cut into 1½" x 2" pieces. Mix squid with cornstarch, dry sherry, salt, and egg white in a bowl.

2. Soak black fungus in hot water for 5 minutes until softened. Rinse and wash sand away. Discard stems and chop into pieces.

3. Mix seasoning sauce in a small bowl and set aside.

4. Heat wok over high heat; add oil. When oil is warm (320°F), stir-fry squid until it begins to curl and turn white. In colander, over a bowl, drain squid.**

5. Reheat 1 TBS drained oil in same wok over medium-high heat. Stir-fry green onion, ginger, garlic, and hot bean sauce until fragrant. Add water chestnuts, black fungus, and snow peas; stir lightly. Add seasoning sauce and squid. Stir over high heat and mix well. Serve hot.

* ¼ cup black mushrooms or fresh mushrooms may be substituted for black fungus.

** You can plunge squid into boiling water instead of sealing in oil before stir-frying with vegetables.

蝦多磷鈣益腦補血

"Shrimp contains phosphorus and calcium which are good for the brain and blood."

芹菜炒魷魚

SAUTEED SQUID WITH CELERY

Squid is economical and nutritious. An excellent way to cook squid is to plunge it into boiling water first, then stir-fry with vegetables.

Serves 4   **Difficulty level 3**

6	oz celery		
3/4	lb fresh squid		
4	TBS salad oil		
5-6	slices ginger, shredded		
5-6	slices carrot, shredded		
2	cloves garlic, chopped		

SEASONING SAUCE:

3	TBS chicken stock
2	TBS soy sauce
1	TBS dry sherry
1	tsp salt
1	tsp sesame oil
1/2	tsp cornstarch
1/2	tsp sugar

1. Wash celery and cut into strips about 2" x ½". Plunge celery strips into a large pot with 6 cups of boiling water. Cook for 1 minute. Using a strainer, remove celery from boiling water. Rinse with cold water and set aside.

2. Cut open squid with scissors and remove all material from body. Peel off pink skin and rinse well. Score squid by making diagonal cuts to 2/3 deep on the <u>inside</u> <u>surface</u>, using an angled cut, crisscross fashion. Cut into 1½" x 2½" pieces. Plunge into same boiling water until squid curls and turns slightly white. Do not overcook. Drain and rinse with cold water. Set aside.

3. Mix seasoning sauce in a bowl and set aside.

4. Heat wok over medium-high heat; add 1 TBS oil. Stir-fry celery until tender crisp. Remove, drain, and set aside. Add 3 TBS oil to wok and stir-fry ginger, carrot, and garlic for 30 seconds. Pour in sauce and stir until thickened. Add celery and squid. Stir quickly over high heat to mix well. Serve immediately.

TOFU

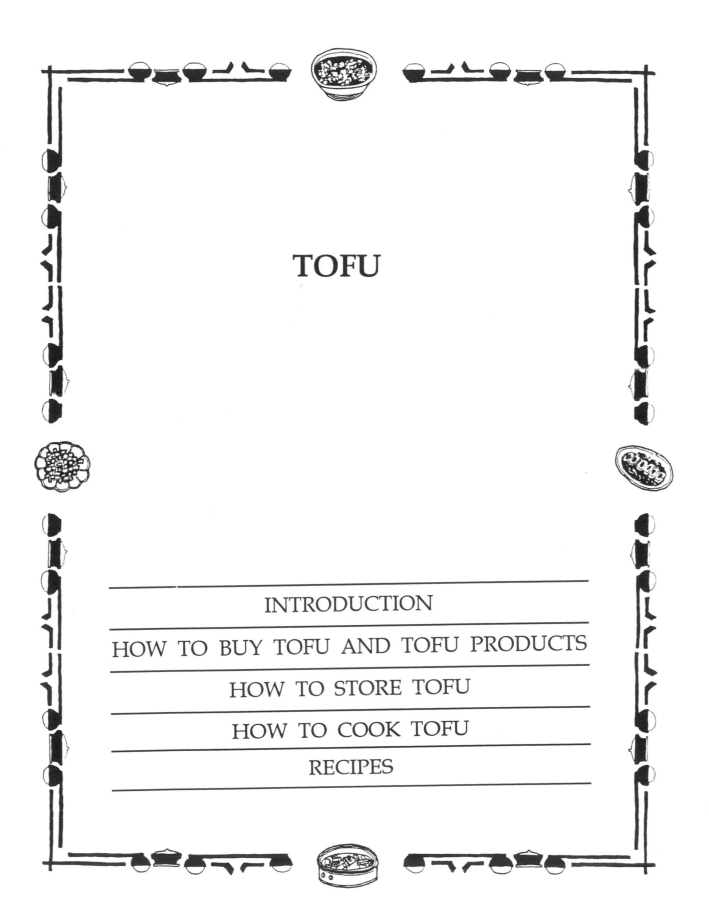

TOFU

INTRODUCTION

Tofu, also known as bean curd, is rich in protein and calcium. Tofu has no cholesterol and is low in fat. Bean curd is made from soybeans using a process similar to the one used for making cottage cheese. First, the soybeans are soaked and then ground into a powder. Water is added to form a puree that is strained through a cloth. Next, the strained puree is heated until boiling. A small amount of gypsum is used to set the tofu before it is poured into a mold. Weights are placed on top of the mold for a few minutes or more, depending on the desired firmness of the finished product. The quality of water used in making tofu determines the tofu's final flavor.

Bean curd is an excellent source of calcium for the elderly and babies. It is soft and can be easily digested. The flavor is mild with a creamy, custard-like texture. Tofu is a good source of protein for vegetarians and for dieters who are trying to cut down on meat intake.

HOW TO BUY TOFU AND TOFU PRODUCTS

You can usually find fresh tofu in boxes and plastic tubs in the refrigerated dairy case of supermarkets. Sometimes tofu is kept with the Chinese vegetables in the produce department. Always read the date on the container to determine freshness. Do not buy frozen or outdated tofu. Tofu is sold in containers by various weights. The firmness of the tofu is usually marked with a color code. Firm tofu is easier to handle and popular for stir-frying and deep-frying. This form of tofu is often cut into four sections. Softer forms of tofu are usually served right out of the container or scrambled with other ingredients.

Chinese grocery stores sell fresh tofu in round tubs. This is an extremely soft tofu and is generally used in soups. Tofu also comes in vacuum-packed boxes which do not need refrigeration. These are handy to have when you cannot buy fresh tofu.

The tastiest kind of tofu is seasoned and baked. Baked savory tofu comes in four flat pieces in a small package. The darker the color, the more flavorful. Once baked, tofu tastes like meat and is often used as a meat substitute. Baked tofu spoils easily and must be refrigerated.

Tofu spaghetti is actually pressed tofu which has been cut into thin strips. It resembles spaghetti but is made from bean curd. Tofu spaghetti should be consumed within a few days after purchase as it does not keep well.

Fried tofu is also available in Oriental grocery stores. Because it takes a long time to deep-fry tofu, it is convenient to purchase tofu already fried. Fried tofu can be stuffed with ground meat and cooked in soup with bean threads and Napa cabbage.

Tofu drinks are as nutritious as low fat milk. Many babies who are allergic to cows' milk can drink this instead. Tofu drink is available plain or sweetened with sugar. Many Chinese enjoy tofu drink in the morning with steamed bread. The drink is usually heated and seasoned with soy sauce and green onions.

Dried sticks and sheets of tofu are available in packages in Chinese grocery stores. Both need to be soaked in warm water and softened before use.

Tofu is also fermented and preserved. In general, preserved tofu is sold in jars with various seasonings added. Some are very salty and spicy and are used as flavorings for many dishes. Others are eaten with porridge or congee for breakfast.

HOW TO STORE TOFU

Tofu must be kept refrigerated. Unopened boxes stay fresh until the printed expiration date. After opening, place tofu in a container filled with fresh cold water and cover tightly. Change the water daily. Try to use opened tofu within a week. Tofu is spoiled if it tastes sour, smells bad, develops mold, or if the storage water has become milky. If tofu turns yellow in color, throw it away.

Tofu may be frozen, but freezing changes the texture, making the tofu spongy and full of holes. Use frozen tofu in dishes like Chinese Fire Pot or Ma-Po's Tofu where the sauce makes the dish taste like meat.

HOW TO COOK TOFU

Since tofu is precooked, it requires little preparation. Just open the box, drain, and eat tofu as is. Or, blanch or parboil to tenderize and sterilize it. Parboiling is especially important if you are serving tofu to babies. Parboiling eliminates the nutty flavor and makes tofu more palatable.

Tofu is quite bland, almost flavorless, and can be seasoned with many different kinds of sauces. The most popular is soy sauce and sesame oil. Tofu can be used in salads, soups, main dishes, and even desserts. It can be served hot or cold and cooked with strongly flavored foods such as meat, seafood, poultry, eggs, and vegetables.

There are many ways to cook tofu. It can be stir-fried, boiled, steamed, deep-fried, braised, baked, and stewed. Often a combination of these cooking methods is used to prepare one dish. Do not overcook tofu. The texture and consistency change when it is cooked too long. Leftover tofu may be reheated in the microwave.

炸 豆 腐

CRISPY TOFU

Crispy tofu tastes like french fries. Dip in Flavored Pepper Salt or hot chili oil and serve as a vegetable. Children like crispy tofu cubes with ketchup or with sugar for dessert.

Serves 6-7   **Difficulty level 1**

1	box (19 oz) firm tofu
1	cup cornstarch
1 1/2	tsp baking powder
3-4	cups salad oil

CONDIMENTS:
1   TBS sugar
1/2   TBS Flavored Pepper Salt
         (recipe on page 64)

1. Drain and cut tofu into ⅔" cubes. Drain well on paper towels.

2. Mix cornstarch and baking powder in a large bowl. Add tofu and toss gently with cornstarch mixture.

3. Heat oil to 375°F over high heat in wok. Fry tofu cubes, a few pieces at a time, until crispy and light brown, about 1½ minutes. Drain on paper towels. Serve hot with sugar and/or Flavored Pepper Salt.

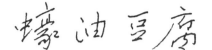

TOFU WITH OYSTER SAUCE

This dish is a favorite with my family. I serve it often with light, stir-fried shrimp and vegetable dishes.

Serves 4-5   **Difficulty level 1**

1	box (19 oz) firm tofu	3	TBS oyster sauce
2	TBS salad oil	1/4	tsp sugar
2	green onions, minced	1	TBS cornstarch mixed
1/2	tsp minced garlic		with 1 TBS water
1	cup chicken stock	1	tsp sesame oil

1. Drain and cut tofu into 3/4" cubes.

2. Heat wok over medium heat; add oil. In warm oil (320°F), add tofu, green onions, and garlic. Stir gently to avoid breaking tofu, until coated with oil. When garlic is fragrant, add stock and bring to a boil. Reduce heat to low; cover and simmer for about 3 minutes.

3. Remove cover; gently stir in oyster sauce and sugar. Over high heat, bring liquid to a boil. Stir in cornstarch mixture and cook until thickened. Sprinkle with sesame oil. Serve hot.

蟹扮豆腐

TOFU WITH CRAB SAUCE

You will love this delicious crab sauce. If you are allergic to crab, use imitation crab meat which is made with fish.

Serves 4-5   **Difficulty level 1**

1	box (19 oz) firm tofu	1	tsp salt
3	TBS salad oil	1	TBS cornstarch mixed
1/2	TBS chopped ginger		with 1 TBS water
1/2	cup (6 oz) cooked crab meat	1	egg white, beaten
1/2	TBS dry sherry	2	TBS chopped green onion
1	cup chicken stock	1	tsp sesame oil

1. Drain and cut tofu into ½" x 1" squares.

2. In a large pot, in 6 cups boiling water, parboil tofu for 1 minute. Drain well.

3. Heat wok over medium-high heat; add oil. Stir-fry ginger; add crab meat and stir for a few seconds. Quickly add sherry, then chicken stock. Gently add tofu and salt. Cook over low heat for about 3 minutes. Slowly stir in cornstarch mixture and cook until thickened. Stir in beaten egg white until blended. Remove from heat. Place in deep platter; sprinkle with green onions and sesame oil. Serve hot.

冬菇豆腐

MUSHROOMS WITH TOFU

Fresh button mushrooms are not readily available in China. They are often imported into China in cans and known as champignon.

Serves 4-5   **Difficulty level 1**

1	can (4 oz) mushrooms		1	tsp minced garlic
1	box (19 oz) tofu		1	TBS soy sauce
1/2	TBS cornstarch		3/4	tsp salt
3	TBS cold water		1	TBS minced green onion
2	TBS salad oil		1	tsp sesame oil

1. Drain canned mushrooms and save the liquid.

2. Drain and cut tofu into ½" x 1" squares.

3. Mix cornstarch with drained mushroom liquid in a small bowl; stir in water.

4. Heat wok over medium heat; add oil. Stir-fry garlic and mushrooms for 2 minutes. Add tofu, soy sauce, and salt; cook 3 minutes stirring gently until liquid is reduced. Stir in cornstarch mixture and cook until thickened. Sprinkle with green onion and sesame oil. Serve hot.

BAKED SAVORY TOFU WITH SPINACH

When I was pregnant, this was the dish I craved the most because the vegetables are parboiled instead of stir-fried in oil.

Serves 4-6   **Difficulty level 1**

10	oz tender spinach (or watercress, celery, snow peas)
1/4	cup black fungus
1	pkg (6 oz) baked savory tofu or 6 oz fresh mushrooms
2	dried red peppers (optional)

SEASONING SAUCE:

3	garlic cloves, minced
1	TBS soy sauce
1	TBS sesame oil
1/2	tsp salt

1. Wash spinach thoroughly. Remove tough stems. Cut into 2½" pieces. Soak black fungus in hot water for 5 minutes. Wash, drain, and remove stems. Slice black fungus and tofu. Remove tips and seeds of red peppers; mince.

2. Mix seasoning sauce ingredients with dry red pepper in a large bowl and set aside.

3. In a large pot, bring 6 cups of water to a boil over high heat. Plunge spinach, black fungus, and tofu into boiling water for 10 seconds. Drain in a colander and gently pat dry with paper towels. Toss spinach mixture with seasoning sauce. Spoon into a serving platter.

鍋貼豆腐

PAN-FRIED TOFU, BEIJING STYLE

In Beijing, a flat bottom, cast iron pan is used to cook this dish. You can pan-fry tofu ahead and keep it warm in a low oven until ready to serve. This tofu dish resembles French toast.

Serves 5   **Difficulty level 2**

1	box (19 oz) firm tofu	**SEASONING SAUCE:**	
1/2	cup flour	1/3	cup chicken stock
1	large egg, beaten	1	TBS soy sauce
3	TBS salad oil	1	TBS dry sherry
2	TBS chopped green onion	1	tsp sesame oil
1/2	TBS chopped ginger	1/2	tsp salt
		1/2	tsp sugar

1. Drain and cut tofu into 2½" x 1" x ½" pieces. Place on paper towels and cover with more paper towels to remove excess moisture. If tofu is very soft and wet, repeat several times with fresh towels. Dredge lightly with flour; dip into the beaten egg.

2. Mix seasoning sauce in a measuring cup and set aside.

3. Heat a 12", non-stick, flat bottom pan over medium-high heat; then add oil. Arrange tofu pieces evenly on bottom of pan. Reduce heat to medium; fry for 1 minute until golden in color. Turn and continue frying until golden brown.

4. Pierce tofu with a fork. Sprinkle with green onion and ginger. Pour seasoning sauce over tofu. Cook over low heat until all the sauce is absorbed, about 5 minutes.

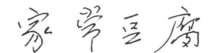

SAUTEED TOFU, FAMILY STYLE

Many people like this tofu dish because it tastes like meat. You may fry the tofu the day before and saute it just before serving.

Serves 4-5   **Difficulty level 2**

1	box (19 oz) firm tofu	1	tsp salt
2-3	cups salad oil	1	tsp sugar
3	oz ground pork or beef	1	TBS cornstarch mixed
1	TBS minced garlic		with 1 TBS water
1	tsp chopped ginger	1	TBS chopped green onion
1	TBS hot bean sauce	1	tsp sesame oil
1/2	cup chicken stock		

1. Drain and cut tofu horizontally into ½" thick squares. Cut each square diagonally into two triangles. Drain tofu on paper towels.

2. Heat oil to 375°F over high heat in wok. Fry tofu, a few pieces at a time, until light brown, about 5-10 minutes. Remove tofu from wok and drain on paper towels. Drain oil.

3. Reheat 2 TBS of drained oil in same wok over medium-high heat. Stir-fry ground meat. Add garlic and ginger; stir in hot bean sauce. Add stock and tofu; bring to a boil. Cover wok and cook over low heat for a few minutes. Add salt and sugar. Stir in cornstarch mixture and cook until thickened. Sprinkle with green onion and sesame oil. Serve hot.

蝦仁豆腐

TOFU WITH SHRIMP, TOMATO, AND GREEN PEAS

This is an inexpensive main dish with a colorful combination of ingredients. This dish is perfect served over steamed rice.

Serves 4-6   **Difficulty level 2**

1/4	lb raw, medium-sized shrimp	3	TBS salad oil
1/2	TBS cornstarch	1	green onion, chopped
1	tsp dry sherry	6	slices ginger
1/4	tsp salt	1/3	cup fresh mushrooms, sliced

SEASONING SAUCE:

1	cup chicken stock	2	cups firm tofu, cut 1/2" cubes
1	TBS soy sauce	1	tomato, diced
1	tsp salt	1/3	cup green peas
1	tsp sugar	1 1/2	TBS cornstarch mixed with 2 TBS water
1/4	tsp black pepper	1/2	TBS sesame oil

1. Wash, drain, and shell shrimp. With knife, butterfly and devein shrimp. Mix shrimp with cornstarch, sherry, and salt in a small bowl.

2. Mix seasoning sauce in a large measuring cup and set aside.

3. Heat wok over high heat; add oil. In warm oil (320°F), add shrimp. Stir constantly for 30 seconds until shrimp begins to turn pink; remove shrimp.

4. In remaining oil, stir-fry green onion and ginger until fragrant. Add mushrooms and toss to coat with oil. Add seasoning sauce and bring to a boil. Add tofu, tomato, and peas. Return to boiling and cook for 2 minutes over medium heat. Add shrimp. Stir in cornstarch mixture and cook until thickened. Add sesame oil. Serve hot.

麻菇豆腐

MA-PO'S TOFU WITH HOT SAUCE

This dish is named after a widow who was known as Ma-Po, meaning freckled lady. After her husband's death she supported herself by selling this dish which has become everyone's favorite. Ma-Po's Tofu may be cooked ahead and reheated in a microwave.

Serves 4-5 **Difficulty level 2**

1/4	lb ground pork or beef	2/3	cup chicken stock
1	TBS soy sauce	1	tsp salt
1	TBS dry sherry	2	tsp cornstarch mixed with 1 TBS water
1/2	tsp sugar		
1	box (19 oz) firm tofu	1	TBS chopped green onion
3	TBS salad oil	1	tsp sesame oil
1	tsp chopped garlic	1	tsp Szechuan peppercorn powder or five spice powder
1-2	TBS hot bean sauce		

1. Combine ground meat, soy sauce, sherry, and sugar in a small bowl. Mix well.

2. Drain and cut tofu into ½" cubes. In a large pot, in 6 cups boiling water, parboil tofu for 1 minute. Drain well.

3. Heat wok over medium-high heat; add oil. Stir-fry meat mixture until cooked. Add garlic; stir in hot bean sauce. Add stock, salt, and tofu. Bring to a boil and cook for 3 minutes over medium heat.* Stir in cornstarch mixture and cook until thickened. Sprinkle with green onion, sesame oil, and Szechuan peppercorn powder; mix lightly. Serve hot.

* For additional color, add ¼ cup of peas.

红烧豆腐

BRAISED TOFU WITH HAM

The ham in this dish makes the tofu taste exceptionally good. The best ham in China is from Yunan province. It has a flavor similar to Virginia Smithfield ham and Italian prosciutto.

Serves 4-5   **Difficulty level 2**

1	box (19 oz) firm tofu	3	TBS salad oil
3	black mushrooms	10	slices bamboo shoots
2	green onions	10	slices carrots
SEASONING SAUCE:		6	slices ham (2" x 1" x 1/8")
1	cup chicken stock	1	TBS cornstarch mixed
2	TBS soy sauce		with 1 TBS water
1	tsp sugar		

1. Drain and cut tofu into ½" x 1" squares. In a large pot, in 6 cups boiling water, parboil tofu for 1 minute. Drain well.

2. Soak black mushrooms in warm water for 15 minutes. Cut off stems; then cut mushroom caps in half. Cut green onions into 1" pieces.

3. Mix seasoning sauce in a large measuring cup and set aside.

4. Heat oil in wok over medium-high heat. Stir-fry green onions until coated with oil. Add black mushrooms, bamboo shoots, carrots, and ham. Stir-fry for 10 seconds. Add seasoning sauce and bring to a boil. Carefully stir in tofu; simmer for 10 minutes. Gently stir in cornstarch mixture and cook until thickened. Serve hot.

素炒豆腐干

BAKED SAVORY TOFU WITH MIXED VEGETABLES

This dish tastes good hot or cold. It can be served over rice or noodles to make a one dish meal.

Serves 4-6   **Difficulty level 2**

4	black mushrooms	2	TBS salad oil
1	medium-sized carrot	1/2	cup shredded bamboo shoots
4	oz celery	1	green onion, shredded
2	oz ham or canned mushrooms	1/2	tsp salt
1	pkg (6 oz) baked savory tofu	1/4	tsp sugar
4	oz bean sprouts	1	TBS sesame oil

1. Soak black mushrooms in warm water for 15 minutes. Cut off stems and shred mushroom caps.

2. Peel and cut off ends of carrot and celery. Shred carrot, celery, ham, and tofu into bean sprout size. Wash and remove tails of bean sprouts; drain well.

3. Heat oil in wok over medium heat. Stir-fry carrot and celery for 1-2 minutes. Add black mushrooms, bamboo shoots, ham, tofu, and green onion; mix well. Add bean sprouts; season with salt and sugar. Stir and sprinkle with sesame oil. Serve hot or cold.

STUFFED TOFU, CANTONESE STYLE

This dish resembles little pocket sandwiches and is flavored with a wonderful sauce.

Serves 4   **Difficulty level 3**

1	box (19 oz) firm tofu	1/4	cup salad oil
1	TBS dried shrimp or ham	1	cup chicken stock
3	oz fish fillet, chopped*	2	TBS oyster sauce
3	oz ground pork or beef	1/2	TBS cornstarch mixed
1/2	TBS green onion, chopped		with 1 TBS water
1/2	TBS dry sherry	1	TBS shredded green onion
1/2	TBS soy sauce	parsley for garnish	
1	tsp cornstarch		
1/4	tsp salt		

1. Lay 4 pieces of tofu on paper towels. Place a heavy cutting board on tofu pieces. Press out as much liquid as possible by placing a pot of water on top of the board. Press tofu for ½-1 hour. Cut each piece diagonally to make 8 triangles.

2. Meanwhile, soak dried shrimp in cold water for 15 minutes. Drain and save shrimp liquid. Chop shrimp finely. Mix shrimp with next 7 ingredients and 1 TBS reserved shrimp liquid. With a small knife, cut a slit in the side of each tofu triangle. Stuff each slit with fish mixture.

3. Heat oil in non-stick pan over medium heat. Pan-fry tofu with stuffing side down for about 2 minutes or until golden brown. Pour off extra oil; add stock. Cover and simmer for 5 minutes, turning tofu over for even cooking. Remove tofu to a large serving plate; cover and keep warm.

4. Stir oyster sauce and cornstarch mixture into liquid in pan; cook until thickened. Sprinkle with shredded green onion; pour sauce over tofu. Garnish with parsley. Serve hot.

* Any white fish fillets will do, such as sole, cod, and bass.

青菜能益氣生津闲胃補空

"Vegetables will create energy, improve the appetite,
and enhance the spirit."

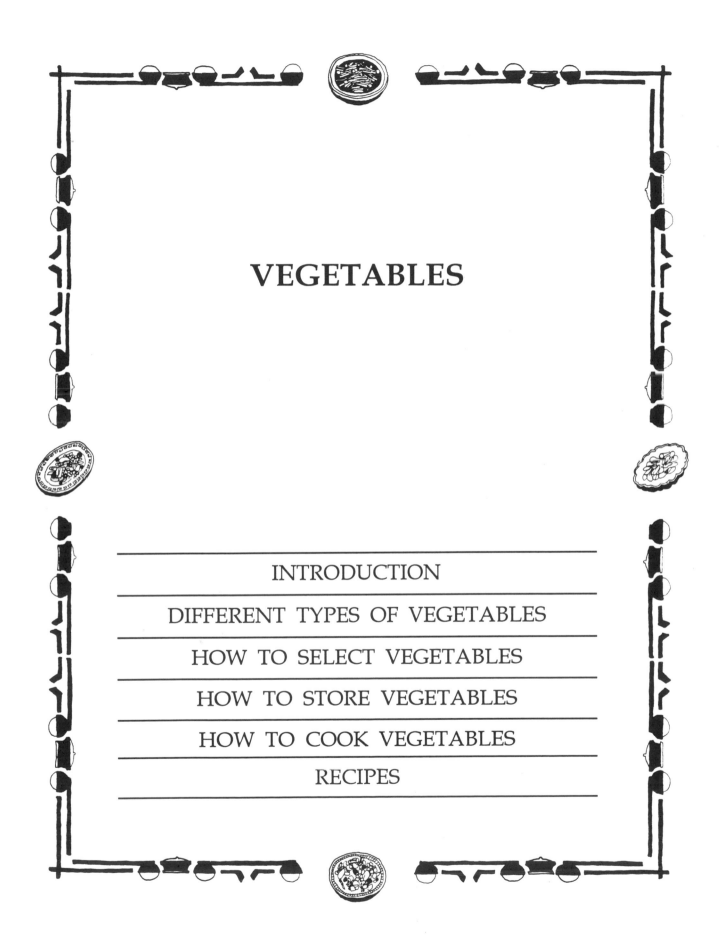

VEGETABLES

VEGETABLES

INTRODUCTION

Vegetables are an essential part of our daily food choices. They are high in fiber and have no cholesterol. In China vegetables are served at every meal. For breakfast, pickled vegetables are often eaten with a large bowl of steaming porridge. Lunch and dinner always include one or two dishes of greens. Much time and effort is put into preparing vegetables that look as attractive and taste as delicious as other dishes.

My mother was a vegetarian due to her Buddhist religion. She made tofu and sprouted beans at home. She often made delicious and appetizing meals using all vegetarian ingredients. If you ever have a chance to visit the Orient, you should try to attend a banquet at a Buddhist Temple. You will be surprised how many dishes look and taste like meat but are actually made from vegetables. One famous dish is called the Vegetarian Goose. It comes wrapped in tofu skin and is stuffed with all kinds of vegetables.

DIFFERENT TYPES OF VEGETABLES

There are three major groups of vegetables:

1. **Root vegetables** — turnips, daikon, carrots, potatoes, onions, water chestnuts, ginger, and bamboo shoots.

2. **Leafy vegetables** — spinach; Napa cabbage, sometimes called Chinese cabbage or celery cabbage; bok choy; baby bok choy; round cabbage; Chinese green cabbage, also sold as "Sin Kan Tsai" or heart of cabbage; broccoli; celery; lettuce; watercress; and cilantro.

3. **Fruit vegetables** — tomatoes, cucumbers, eggplant, winter melon, bitter melon, string beans, and peas.

HOW TO SELECT VEGETABLES

In selecting root vegetables, look for those with few blemishes and bruises. Buy shiny ones, which are fresher than wrinkled ones. This is especially true with ginger. In general, the smaller vegetables are younger and more tender.

Pick green leafy vegetables that are small and tender, versus old and tough. If you are buying cabbage or lettuce, hold it in your hand to see if it is heavy and firm. Avoid brown or wilted leaves.

In buying fruit vegetables, look for plumpness and firmness. The more intense the color, the better. Avoid buying ones that are bruised or wrinkled. They have been sitting around too long. Usually the smaller the fruit vegetable, the more tender, except for tomatoes.

HOW TO STORE VEGETABLES

Root vegetables do not spoil quickly. Store them in a dry, cool place or in the refrigerator. They will keep for more than a week or two when stored this way. Never wash vegetables until ready to use.

Leafy vegetables should be used within a week. Their vitamin content diminishes from exposure to both air and sunlight. Again, never wash them until ready to use. If the leaves are very damp when you first bring them home from the grocery store, pat dry with paper toweling before putting them in the vegetable drawer of the refrigerator.

Fruit vegetables keep longer in the refrigerator than the leafy kind. Some of them are waxed and spoil less readily than vegetables that are not waxed. Once cut, fruit vegetables should be cooked and eaten as soon as possible.

HOW TO COOK VEGETABLES

When I was in college, I took a basic cooking class in Home Economics School. We tested vegetables cooked many different ways: steaming, sauteing, stir-frying, and boiling. Almost all students who sampled the dishes picked stir-fried vegetables as their favorite. It is no wonder that the Chinese have used this method to cook their vegetables for thousands of years.

When stir-frying vegetables, it is important to wash them first and drain well. This is especially true with leafy vegetables, such as spinach. The wok need not be piping hot before you add your cooking oil since vegetables usually do not stick to the wok. Adding salt and ginger first will prevent splattering and will also make the oil more fragrant and seasoned. Always add the stems before the rest, since they require a longer cooking time. After the vegetables are well coated with oil, add a little water or stock and steam them covered over low heat for a few minutes. Steaming softens tough vegetables. Be careful not to over cook! Two to three minutes of steaming is enough for many vegetables. Test doneness by sampling a stem or a tough piece. If it is soft, then add seasonings, such as soy sauce and a dash of sugar. Serve immediately. Never reheat vegetables or leave them covered to keep warm for too long. The beautiful green color will turn yellow. If you must reheat, use a microwave. The texture of the vegetables will not change much, but the color may not be as bright.

Another common method of cooking tough vegetables is to parboil them before stir-frying. Parboiling means cooking in a large pot filled with 6-8 cups of boiling water. Drop the vegetables into the water, and let water return to a boil again. Cook the vegetables for a few minutes until softened and the color becomes very intense. Immediately drain and rinse with cold water so that the heat of the hot water will not continue to cook the vegetables. Now they are ready to be stir-fried. The beauty of this method is that you can prepare many different kinds of vegetables in one dish. Each vegetable is parboiled separately. When they are combined together, each one is perfectly tender and the color is very intense. Parboiling can be done earlier in the day. When you are ready to serve the vegetables, you just stir-fry in oil and add seasonings. There is no need to cover and steam, because the vegetables are already softened.

Some vegetables are so tender that they do not need to be steamed or parboiled. Good examples are spinach, lettuce, cucumber, tomatoes and snow peas. These only need to be stir-fried in a little oil for a few minutes before serving.

BASIC STIR-FRIED VEGETABLES

I have included this recipe to allow you to enjoy eating many different kinds of vegetables daily.

Serves 4   **Difficulty Level 1**

1	lb vegetables
2	TBS salad oil
1/2	tsp salt
2	slices ginger
1/4	cup chicken stock or water
1	TBS soy sauce
1/2	tsp sugar

1. Prepare vegetables for cooking as described on the following page.

2. Heat oil in wok or a large frying pan, over medium-high heat. Add salt, then ginger and stir-fry a few times. Add vegetables. Stir-fry to coat with oil and heat through.

3. Add stock or water and bring to a boil. Cover and simmer over medium heat until vegetables are tender. (See instructions for cooking each kind of vegetable listed below.)

4. Uncover; gently stir in soy sauce and sugar. Serve hot.

INSTRUCTIONS FOR PREPARING VEGETABLES:

Asparagus: Bend each stalk back until tough root end snaps away. Discard ends. Cut stalks diagonally in 1"-1½" sections. In step 3, cook 2-3 minutes.

Broccoli: Break head into small flowerets. Trim away tough ends and peel stems. Cut stems diagonally into ½" slices. In step 3, cook 3 minutes. Continue cooking uncovered, 1 minute more in step 4.

Cauliflower: Remove leaves and core. Break head into small flowerets. In step 3, cook 3 minutes.

Celery: Trim off leaves and tough stem ends. Cut stalks diagonally in ½" sections. In step 3, cook 2-3 minutes.

Napa Cabbage: Discard tough outer leaves. Cut cabbage into 1½" pieces. Separate the stalks and leaves. In step 2, stir-fry stalks first, then add leaves. In step 3, cook about 2-3 minutes.

Snow Peas: Snap off both ends and remove strings. Leave whole, if tender; if not, cut in half diagonally. In step 3, cook 1-2 minutes.

Spinach: Wash thoroughly, and drain well. Remove tough stems. Cut spinach into 2" pieces. Omit steps 3 and 4. At the end of step 2, sprinkle with the soy sauce and sugar, and cook only until leaves turn dark green and soft.

String Beans: Stem; then cut or break into 1"-2" sections. In step 2, add a crushed garlic clove if you wish. In step 3, cook 4-5 minutes.

You may combine several vegetables together in one dish. The following is a chart to help you select different types of vegetables that go well together. For best results, try to combine vegetables with similar cooking times, such as broccoli, cauliflower, and carrots.

BASIC STIR-FRIED VEGETABLES SIMMERING TIME CHART

HARD VEGETABLES

4-5 minutes of simmering, covered:

      string beans
      potatoes
      swiss chard
      peas in the pod

3 minutes of simmering, covered:

      broccoli
      cauliflower
      carrots
      turnips
      cabbage
      black mushrooms

SEMI-HARD VEGETABLES

2-3 minutes of simmering, covered:

asparagus	mustard cabbage
Napa cabbage	lotus roots
celery	onion
bamboo shoots	peppers
brussels sprouts	water chestnuts

1-2 minutes of simmering, covered:

      snow peas
      mushrooms
      zucchini
      cucumber

SOFT VEGETABLES

No need to simmer, covered:

      spinach
      lettuce
      watercress
      tomatoes
      bean sprouts

炒 豆 芽

BEAN SPROUTS WITH GREEN ONION

Mung bean sprouts are more nutritious and delicious than beans because sprouting transforms starch into tender shoots that are loaded with vitamins and natural sugars.

Serves 4-6   **Difficulty level 1**

1	lb bean sprouts	1	green onion, shredded
2	TBS salad oil	1/4	cup shredded carrots
1	tsp salt	1/4	tsp sesame oil

1. Wash and remove tails of bean sprouts. Drain well.

2. Heat oil in wok over high heat. Add salt, green onion, and carrots, and stir-fry for 1 minute. Add bean sprouts, and stir until transparent and thoroughly mixed. Sprinkle with sesame oil. Serve hot or cold.

SNOW PEAS WITH MUSHROOMS AND BAMBOO SHOOTS

This simple, elegant dish can be served with any main dish.

Serves 4-5   **Difficulty level 1**

6	black mushrooms
	    or canned mushrooms
		1/2	cup sliced bamboo shoots
			    or water chestnuts

1	lb snow peas	1	tsp salt
2	TBS salad oil	1/4	tsp sugar

1. Soak mushrooms in warm water for 15 minutes. Save liquid for stock. Cut off stems and cut mushroom caps in half. Snap off both ends of snow peas and remove strings. Wash and drain well.

2. Heat oil in wok over high heat. Add mushrooms and bamboo shoots; stir-fry for 2 minutes. Add snow peas, salt, sugar, and 2 TBS of mushroom liquid. Stir constantly for about 2 minutes. Serve hot.

GREEN BEANS WITH WATER CHESTNUTS

The crispness of green beans and water chestnuts goes especially well with juicy, tender seafood.

Serves 4   **Difficulty level 1**

1	lb green beans
2	TBS salad oil
10	water chestnuts cut into 1/4" slices*
1/2-1	tsp salt
1/2	tsp sugar
1/3	cup chicken stock
1	TBS soy sauce
1	tsp cornstarch mixed with 1 TBS of chicken stock

1. Wash beans. Snap off ends and remove strings. Cut beans into 2" lengths.

2. Heat oil in wok over medium-high heat. Add beans and stir-fry for 3 minutes. Add water chestnuts, salt, and sugar; and stir. Add stock. Cover and cook over moderate heat for 2-3 minutes until beans are tender-crisp. Stir in soy sauce and cornstarch mixture. Cook until vegetables are coated with a light, clear glaze. Serve hot.

* 1/2 cup sliced fresh mushrooms may be substituted for water chestnuts.

慷油炒菜,

BROCCOLI WITH OYSTER SAUCE

My family loves broccoli cooked with oyster sauce. When my son was little he called them "little green trees."

Serves 6   **Difficulty level 1**

2	lb fresh broccoli*	
2	TBS salad oil	
2	slices ginger	
1	tsp cornstarch mixed with	
	1 TBS water	

SEASONING SAUCE:
1/4	cup chicken stock
2	TBS oyster sauce
1	tsp sugar
1/2	tsp salt

1. Wash broccoli. Trim away tough ends and peel stems. Cut broccoli into 3" long and 3/4" wide pieces.

2. Mix seasoning sauce in a measuring cup and set aside.

3. Heat oil in wok over medium-high heat. Add ginger, then broccoli stalks. Stir-fry about 1 minute to coat pieces thoroughly with oil. Stir in seasoning sauce, mixing well. Cover wok and cook over medium heat for 2-3 minutes until tender-crisp. Stir in cornstarch mixture and cook until broccoli is coated with a light, clear glaze. Serve hot.

* Asparagus may be substituted for broccoli.

奶油白菜

BOK CHOY WITH CREAM SAUCE

This dish is often served at the end of a banquet. The delicate and creamy white sauce over the green vegetable is a perfect way to cleanse the palate and end a meal.

Serves 4-5 **Difficulty level 1**

1	lb bok choy or Napa cabbage	1	tsp salt
1/4	cup cold milk	1/4	tsp sugar
1	TBS cornstarch	3/4	cup chicken stock
2	TBS salad oil	2	TBS minced, cooked ham

1. Trim off wilted leaves and root ends of vegetable. Separate stalks and wash them under cold running water. Cut into 1" pieces.

2. Combine milk with cornstarch in a measuring cup.

3. Heat oil in wok over medium-high heat. Add vegetable and stir-fry for about 1 minute. Sprinkle with salt and sugar; add stock and stir well. Bring stock to a boil. Cover wok and turn heat to low; simmer for 4-5 minutes. Transfer vegetable with a slotted spoon to a heated platter.

4. Over medium-high heat bring cooking liquid to a boil. Stir in cornstarch mixture until sauce thickens. Pour sauce over vegetable. Sprinkle with ham and serve hot.

五色素菜

STIR-FRIED VEGETABLES WITH BABY CORN

Cantonese are famous for their stir-fry dishes with oyster sauce. This vegetable dish is typical of that region.

Serves 4-6   **Difficulty level 1**

1	medium-sized carrot	**SEASONING SAUCE:**
1	stalk celery	3/4 cup chicken stock
1/2	onion	1 TBS oyster sauce
1	cup canned baby corn, drained*	1 tsp soy sauce
1/4	lb snow peas	1/2 tsp sugar
2	TBS salad oil	1/4 tsp black pepper
1/2	tsp salt	
1	cup canned straw mushrooms, drained	
1	TBS cornstarch mixed with 1 TBS chicken stock	

1. Wash and peel carrot and celery. Cut diagonally into 1" thin slices. Peel and cut onion into 3/4" squares. Cut baby corn in half lengthwise. Wash and stem snow peas.

2. Mix seasoning sauce in a measuring cup and set aside.

3. Heat oil in wok over medium-high heat. Add salt. Add carrots and stir-fry for 30 seconds. Add celery and onion and stir-fry until tender-crisp, about 45 seconds. Add baby corn, snow peas, and straw mushrooms. Stir-fry for 30 seconds. Stir in seasoning sauce and mix well. Stir in cornstarch mixture. Heat just until sauce comes to a boil and thickens. Serve hot.

* Fresh or canned mushrooms may be substituted for baby corn.

洋菇素菜

BRAISED MUSHROOMS WITH SPINACH

This is actually two dishes combined into one, but each can be served separately. Braised mushrooms can be served cold as an appetizer with toothpicks. The cooked spinach can be served as a side dish.

Serves 4-5   **Difficulty level 1**

1	lb fresh mushrooms	2	TBS soy sauce
2	bunches fresh spinach	2	tsp sugar
1	cup salad oil	1	tsp salt

1. Rinse and drain mushrooms. Cut a thin slice from each stem end.

2. Wash spinach thoroughly and drain well. Remove tough stems. Cut spinach in half.

3. Heat oil to 350°F in wok over medium-high heat. Fry mushrooms until caps shrink slightly, about 1-2 minutes. Add soy sauce and sugar; stir until well mixed. Cover and cook over low heat for 10 minutes, stirring once or twice for even coloring. Place colander over a bowl; drain mushrooms. Reserve oil mixture.

4. Return 2 TBS of drained oil mixture to the same wok. Add salt and spinach. Stir-fry until leaves turn dark green. Place spinach around the edge of the serving platter. Spoon mushrooms into the center. Serve hot.

蟹油烤菜

BAKED NAPA CABBAGE WITH CRAB SAUCE

This dish can be stir-fried a day ahead and baked in the oven just before serving. This is a great party platter with no last minute fuss.

Serves 5-6   **Difficulty level 2**

1 1/2	lb Napa cabbage	3	TBS salad oil
2	TBS salad oil	3	TBS flour
1 1/2	tsp salt	1	can (14 1/2 oz) chicken broth
1	tsp sugar	3	TBS milk
1/2	cup cooked crab meat		

1. Remove cabbage leaves. Wash and cut into 2" crosswise slices. Then slice into 1" wide strips (leafy part may be cut a little wider). Preheat oven to 400°F.*

2. Heat 2 TBS oil in wok over medium-high heat. Add cabbage stems and stir-fry for about 1 minute until just softened. Add cabbage leaves and continue stir-frying just until soft. Season with salt and sugar; cook until half tender. Drain cabbage in a strainer and discard the liquid. Clean wok.

3. In cleaned wok, heat 3 TBS of oil to warm (260°F) over medium heat. Stir in flour and cook a few seconds. Slowly stir in chicken broth until thickened. Add crab meat; mix well. Turn off heat. Add milk, mixing thoroughly. Remove half of sauce to a bowl and set aside.

4. Pour cooked cabbage into wok with sauce and mix. Spoon into 8" square, heat-proof dish. Pour reserved sauce over top.** Place in preheated oven, and bake for 20 minutes or until surface turns slightly golden brown. Serve hot.

* If stir-frying cabbage ahead, preheat oven 10 minutes before baking to serve.

** If making a day ahead, refrigerate here.

粉絲四季豆

CHINESE STRING BEANS WITH BEAN THREADS

Chinese string beans are 1-3 feet in length. Otherwise, they resemble green beans. By first sealing in oil, the beans become intense in color and soft in texture. If you like, you can parboil beans in boiling water instead of cooking in oil in step 4.

Serves 4-6   **Difficulty level 2**

1	lb Chinese string beans	**SEASONING SAUCE:**	
2	oz bean threads*	1	cup chicken stock
1	cup salad oil	1	TBS soy sauce
3	oz ground pork or beef	1	tsp salt
1	TBS chopped green onion	1/2	tsp sesame oil
		1/4	tsp sugar

1. Wash beans. Snap off ends and remove strings. Cut beans into 2" lengths.

2. Soak bean threads in warm water for 10 minutes. Rinse and drain. Use scissors to cut threads into 6"-8" lengths.

3. Mix seasoning sauce in a measuring cup and set aside.

4. Heat oil in wok over high heat. Add beans and stir-fry until soft, about 3 minutes. Place colander over a bowl; drain beans.

5. Reheat 2 TBS of drained oil in the same wok over medium-high heat. Add ground meat and stir. Add green onion and string beans, stirring until mixed. Add seasoning sauce and bring to boil. Cook for 3 minutes. Add bean threads and cook, over high heat, until the liquid is absorbed.

* Bean threads must be softened first before stir-frying with the green beans. Add bean threads last; otherwise, they will soak up all the sauce.

SPICY EGGPLANT, SZECHUAN STYLE

Chinese eggplant is tender and small in size. It needs no peeling. This spicy dish is excellent served hot or cold.

Serves 4-6   **Difficulty level 2**

4	eggplants (about 12 oz)	**SEASONING SAUCE:**	
2	cups salad oil	1/2	cup chicken stock
1	tsp chopped garlic	2	TBS soy sauce
1/2	TBS chopped ginger	1	tsp sugar
1	TBS hot bean sauce	1/2	tsp salt
1/2	TBS rice vinegar		
1/2	TBS sesame oil		
1	TBS chopped green onion		

1. Wash and cut off ends of eggplant. Without peeling, cut into thumb-sized pieces.

2. Mix seasoning sauce in a measuring cup and set aside.

3. Heat oil to 375°F in wok over high heat. Add eggplant; turn heat to medium-low. Stir-fry until soft, about 2-3 minutes. Press eggplant against wok to squeeze out excess oil. Remove from wok and drain on paper towels. Drain oil.

4. Reheat 1 TBS of drained oil in the same wok over medium-high heat. Add garlic and ginger; stir until fragrant. Add hot bean sauce; stir for a few seconds. Add seasoning sauce and bring to a boil. Add eggplant and cook for about 1 minute until sauce is absorbed. Add vinegar and sesame oil; stir until mixed. Sprinkle with green onion. Mix carefully and serve hot or cold.

SAUTEED VEGETABLE MEDLEY

This is a deluxe vegetarian feast. If you like the sauce, you can use it for other vegetable combinations.

Serves 6-8   **Difficulty level 3**

1	dried tofu stick*	**SEASONING SAUCE:**	
6	black mushrooms	1/2	cup soup stock
1/4	lb cauliflower	2	TBS soy sauce
1/4	lb broccoli	1/2	TBS sesame oil
10	small mushrooms	1	tsp salt
1/4	lb round cabbage	1	tsp sugar
1/2	cup bamboo shoots or bell pepper	1	tsp cornstarch
1	carrot		
1/4	lb celery		
1	small zucchini		
10	baby corn, drained		
3	TBS salad oil		

1. In a large pot, bring 10-12 cups of water to a boil over high heat. Break tofu stick into 1" pieces. Cook in boiling water for 20-30 minutes until softened. Remove with slotted spoon.

2. Meanwhile, soak black mushrooms in warm water for 15 minutes. Cut off stems, and cut mushroom caps into quarters. Wash all vegetables. Cut cauliflower and broccoli into bite-sized pieces. Trim stems of small mushrooms. Cut cabbage into 1" sections. Slice bamboo shoots, carrots, celery, and zucchini into thin pieces. Cut corn lengthwise in half.

3. Mix seasoning sauce in a measuring cup and set aside.

4. To the same pot of boiling water, add cauliflower, broccoli, and carrots; parboil 1 minute. Add celery and zucchini; parboil 2 minutes or until color intensifies. Drain and rinse with cold water.

5. Heat oil in a large wok over medium-high heat. Stir-fry black mushrooms with small mushrooms. Add cabbage, and stir until coated with oil. Add remaining ingredients. Pour in seasoning sauce, and cook until the liquid is reduced. Serve as is or on the Golden Plate.

1 cup of cooked spiral shaped pasta may be used instead of tofu stick.

THE GOLDEN PLATE

For banquets, stir-fried dishes are often served in the Golden Plate. You can use this plate for other dishes, such as Snow Peas with Mushrooms or Vegetables with Baby Corn.

Makes 1 plate   **Difficulty level 2**

15-20   dumpling wrappers
1 TBS cornstarch mixed with 1 TBS water
6-8   cups salad oil for deep-frying

1. On a 10" greased strainer, place dumpling wrappers around the middle (Fig. 1), radiating out to the edge, forming a solid plate (Fig. 2). Glue overlapping edges down with cornstarch mixture. Place a second 10" greased strainer over the dumpling wrappers (Fig. 3).

2. Heat oil to 375°F in a 14" wok over high heat. Fry dumpling wrappers until golden brown (Fig. 4). Remove from strainer carefully with a spatula. Drain well on paper towels.

To make ahead: The Golden Plate may be fried hours ahead and kept crisp in a sealed bag. Before serving, reheat in oven, about 300°F, for 5 minutes.

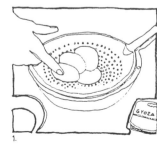
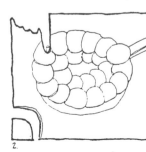
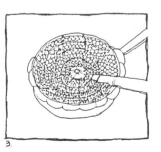
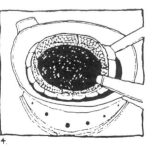

HUNAN ASPARAGUS WITH BLACK BEAN SAUCE

I recommend this dish for those who crave spicy hot food. This flavorful dish goes perfectly with rice.

Serve 6   **Difficulty level 2**

2	lb asparagus	
2	TBS fermented black beans	
2	cloves garlic, minced	
1	TBS minced ginger	
2	TBS salad oil	
1/2	tsp dried red pepper flakes	
1	green onion, cut into 1/4" pieces	
1	TBS cornstarch mixed with 2 TBS water	

SEASONING SAUCE:

1	cup chicken stock
2	TBS soy sauce
1	TBS dry sherry

1. Bend each asparagus stalk back until the tough root end snaps away. Discard ends. Wash and drain. Cut stalks diagonally into 1"-1½" sections.

2. Soak beans in cold water in a small bowl for 5 minutes. Rinse, drain, and mince. Mix with garlic and ginger.

3. Mix seasoning sauce in a measuring cup and set aside.

4. In a large pot, bring 6 cups of water to a boil over high heat. Cook asparagus in boiling water for 1-2 minutes until color intensifies. Drain and rinse with cold water.*

5. Heat oil in wok over high heat. Add black bean mixture and stir-fry a few seconds until fragrant. Immediately add seasoning sauce and bring to a boil. Add asparagus and cook for 1 minute. Add chili flakes and green onions; toss until well mixed. Stir in cornstarch mixture and cook until asparagus is coated with a clear glaze. Serve hot.

* Asparagus can be parboiled earlier in the day.

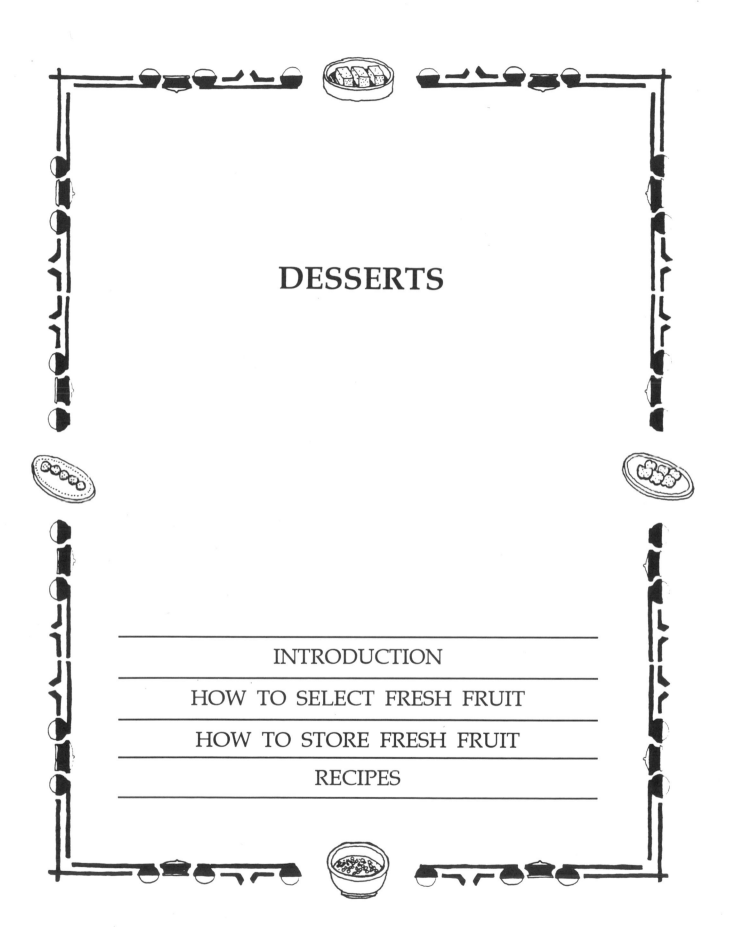

DESSERTS

INTRODUCTION

HOW TO SELECT FRESH FRUIT

HOW TO STORE FRESH FRUIT

RECIPES

DESSERTS

INTRODUCTION

One of my students recently visited China. She told me she had feasted on delicious Chinese food every day. When she came home she was surprised to find she had actually lost weight. I asked if she had many desserts. She said, "Most of the desserts I had in China were fresh fruits." That is one secret to losing weight and yet adding nutrients and fiber to the diet.

In China, sweet desserts are only served on special occasions, such as birthdays, New Year's, or weddings. It is common to finish a meal with slices of oranges, apples, or pears. In fact, it is more satisfying to end a Chinese meal with fresh fruit instead of a sweet dessert. Since most Chinese dishes are well seasoned and usually contain a small amount of sugar to balance out the saltiness of soy sauce, one does not crave sweets but welcomes the tartness of fresh fruit.

For birthdays, a steamed sweet bun in the shape of a peach stuffed with red bean paste is often served. The peach symbolizes long life. Eight Precious Pudding, made with sweet rice and eight varieties of dried fruit, is similar to fruit cake and is a favorite dish to end a formal dinner. Sometimes two desserts are served at a banquet. One is usually fresh fruit or a soupy dessert, such as Almond Float; the other might be solid, like Sweet Rice Balls. Many sweet desserts are made more nutritious by stuffing with red bean paste which is high in fiber.

Cookies are seldom eaten after dinners. They are usually served as a snack between meals. Fortune cookies with messages were invented in Chinatown in New York. In China, these light cookies are flat and round and do not have messages. Sometimes black sesame seeds are added to enhance texture and flavor.

Because Chinese do not use cream or butter in cooking, most desserts in China are low in both cholesterol and calories. Butterfly cookies are a perfect example. They are made with flour, water, salad oil, and powdered sugar.

HOW TO SELECT FRESH FRUIT

Buy fresh fruits when they are in season. They are sweeter and the price is better. Choose unbruised fruit. Bruised fruit spoils faster. Pick up fruit to see if it feels heavy. Heavier fruit is more juicy.

These are guidelines to select top-quality fruits in your market:

APPLES — firm, well shaped and shiny without any bruises

APRICOTS — plump, juicy-looking and tender to touch

BANANAS — yellow ones with some specks are riper than green ones

CANTALOUPE — heavy with a soft end and pleasant aroma

GRAPEFRUIT — heavy and firm to touch

GRAPES — plump and firmly attached to stems

HONEYDEW MELON — heavy with a hollow sound when thumped

KIWIFRUIT — slightly soft to touch indicates sweetness

MANGOES — plump with fresh aroma and slightly soft to touch

ORANGE — heavy and firm to touch

PEACH — soft to touch, avoid green or bruised fruit

PEAR — fairly firm and well shaped without bruises

PINEAPPLE — firm and heavy with sweet aroma

PLUM — soft to touch without any bruises

WATERMELON — heavy with deep, resonant sound when thumped

HOW TO STORE FRESH FRUIT

Storing fresh fruit in the refrigerator will keep it fresh longer. Do not wash fruit until ready to eat. The natural coating on the outside of fruit prevents it from drying out and spoiling. To ripen fruit faster, wash and leave at room temperature or in a brown paper bag. Cut fresh fruits right before serving to prevent loss of nutrients and vitamins. To keep apples, pears, or bananas from turning brown after cutting, pour a little orange or lemon juice over them. To store cut fruit, wrap well with plastic and keep in the refrigerator.

THREE EXOTIC FRUITS ON CRUSHED ICE

Keep a few cans of Chinese fruits in the cupboard. When unexpected guests come for dinner, you will always have a dessert ready to serve.

Serves 5-6   **Difficulty level 1**

1   can (1 lb 4 oz) lychees*
1   can (1 lb 4 oz) loquats*
3   fresh, ripe kiwifruit

1. Open canned fruits. Drain syrup into a small bowl. Arrange fruit in the center of a serving platter covered with crushed ice.

2. Peel and slice kiwifruit into ⅛" thick rounds. Arrange kiwifruit around canned fruits. Pour ¼-½ cup reserved syrup over all fruits. Serve immediately.

* Canned peaches and pears may be substituted for lychees and loquats.

STEAMED PEARS WITH HONEY

Steamed pears are a perfect dessert to serve on a cool night.

Serves 4   **Difficult level 1**

4   ripe pears, Bartlett or Anjou
3-4   TBS honey

1. Peel pears, leaving the stem on. Cut off tops, about 1" down, and reserve as lids. If the pear bottom is not flat, cut off a thin slice so pear will stand upright. Core each pear with a fruit corer making a deep cavity, but do not cut through the bottom.

2. Fill cavities with honey and replace tops.

3. With protective gloves, place pears upright in individual heatproof dishes on rack. Steam in wok or steamer over 1½"-2" of boiling water over medium-high heat until tender, about 15 minutes. Serve pears hot in steamed dishes.

西米橘羹

HOT ORANGE TAPIOCA

The original recipe calls for pearl tapioca which must be soaked for at least 4 hours. This quick and easy version is my son's favorite dessert.

Serves 4-6   **Difficulty level 1**

3	cups cold water
1/2	cup quick-cooking tapioca
1/4	cup sugar
1	large sweet orange*

1. In a 2-quart saucepan, combine water, tapioca, and sugar. Let stand 5 minutes.

2. Peel and cut orange into wedges. Remove white membranes and seeds; reserve juice in bowl.

3. Cook tapioca over medium heat, stirring constantly, until mixture comes to a full boil. Stir in orange wedges and juice. Bring to a boil again. Serve hot.

* 1 can (11 oz) drained mandarin oranges may be substituted for fresh orange.

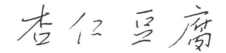

ALMOND FLOAT

In China this dessert is called Almond Tofu because it resembles tofu in color and texture. The original recipe calls for agar agar. Almond Float is refreshing and often served after a lavish banquet. For a large dinner party, double the recipe and make the gelatin a day ahead.

Serves 6   **Difficulty level 1**

1	envelope unflavored gelatin	**GARNISH:**
1/4	cup cold water	fresh strawberries
1/3	cup sugar	sliced kiwifruit
3/4	cup boiling water	Mandarin oranges
3/4	cup milk (homogenized or low fat)	fruit cocktail
1	tsp almond extract	lychees

<u>SYRUP:</u> Mix 1/3 cup sugar with 2 cups cold water and 1/2 tsp almond extract

1. Soften gelatin in cold water in an 8" square pan. Dissolve sugar in boiling water; add to gelatin mixture. Stir thoroughly. Pour in milk and extract. Mix well. Chill until set (at least 2 hours, overnight is preferred). For quick setting, freeze for ½ hour.

2. Cut gelatin into ½" cubes. Use a spatula to scoop cubes into a large serving bowl. Garnish with any of the fruits mentioned above.

3. Pour syrup over gelatin and fruit.* Serve chilled.

* Canned juice may be substituted for syrup. You may also combine 1 cup canned juice with 1 cup syrup, and pour over gelatin and fruit.

蝴 蝶 餅

BUTTERFLY COOKIES

These cookies contain no cholesterol and are low in calories. Keep them crispy and fresh tasting by storing in an airtight container.

Makes 3-4 dozen cookies   **Difficulty level 1**

---

1   pkg (14 oz) wonton wrappers
2-3   cups salad oil
1   cup powdered sugar
1/4   cup cinnamon (optional)

1. Cut wonton wrappers in half. Cut a 1" slit lengthwise through the middle of each rectangle.

2. Stack 2 skins together and pull one end of the rectangle through the slit forming a bow.

3. Heat oil to 350°F in wok. Fry cookies, a few at a time, over medium-high heat until lightly browned on both sides. Drain on paper towel.*

4. Place powdered sugar in a plastic bag. Add cinnamon if you like. Shake a few cookies in the bag at a time, until coated with sugar mixture. Shake off excess sugar. Serve.

* Butterfly cookies, without powdered sugar, are perfect to serve as appetizers with Sweet and Sour Sauce on page 64.

MANGO WEDGES WITH SEEDLESS GRAPES

Mango is in season from May through August. Choose mango with yellowish or orange skin. Let mango ripen at room temperature for several days until the skin yields slightly when touched.

Serves 4   **Difficulty level 1**

2	ripe mangoes
1/2	lb seedless grapes

1. Cut a lengthwise slice from each side of mango as close to long flat seed as possible to make 4 slices. Cut each large slice into 2 wedges. Score the flesh into ¾" squares without cutting through the skin.

2. To serve, place seedless grapes in the center of the platter. Arrange mango wedges around grapes. Serve cold.

PINEAPPLE BOATS WITH CHERRIES

Choose a plump, glossy pineapple with green leaves and sweet aroma. Pineapple is in season all year round.

Serves 4   **Difficulty level 1**

1	ripe pineapple
4	maraschino cherries

1. Cut off half the length of leaves and discard. Cut pineapple in half, then quarters through the crown to the stem end. Cut the core from each quarter. Cut between the fruit and rind, leaving the fruit in the shell. Cut fruit crosswise into ½" thick slices. Push slices slightly out, alternating on each side to form a zig-zag pattern.

2. Put a cherry in the middle of each wedge with a toothpick. Serve chilled.

杏 仁 餅

ALMOND COOKIES

Almond cookies may be baked in advance, wrapped in foil, and frozen. If you are on a low cholesterol diet, use vegetable shortening instead of lard.

Makes 3 dozen cookies   **Difficulty level 2**

1	cup lard, room temperature*	1 1/2	tsp baking powder
1	cup sugar	1/8	tsp salt
1	egg	36	blanched almonds
1	tsp almond extract	1	egg yolk
2 1/2	cups flour	1	TBS water

1. Preheat oven to 350°F.

2. Cream lard and sugar in a mixing bowl. Beat egg and add almond extract. Blend well with sugar mixture.

3. Sift flour with baking powder and salt. Gradually combine flour mixture and sugar mixture with hands. Knead just until dough sticks together.

4. Divide dough into thirds. Cut each third into 12 pieces. With hands, form pieces into small balls and flatten into 1½" rounds.

5. Arrange cookies about 1" apart on greased cookie sheets. Press a whole almond into each cookie. In small bowl, mix egg yolk and water. Brush cookies with egg mixture. Bake until slightly golden, about 15 minutes. Cool on rack.

* Vegetable shortening may be substituted for lard.

SESAME SEED COOKIES

Chinese like to use sesame seeds in desserts because they add texture and flavor. Store these cookies in a tightly covered container.

Makes 7 dozen cookies   **Difficulty level 2**

1	tsp salad oil		2	cups flour
2 1/2	TBS white sesame seeds		1	tsp baking powder
1	cup sugar		1/2	tsp nutmeg
1/2	cup lard (room temperature)*		1/8	tsp salt
1	egg, beaten			

1. Heat oil in a small skillet. Toast sesame seeds over medium heat until golden, stirring frequently. Set aside.

2. Cream sugar and lard in a bowl. Add egg and blend well. Stir in 1½ TBS of toasted sesame seeds.

3. Sift flour with baking powder, nutmeg, and salt. Gradually add flour mixture to sugar mixture until well blended. Knead dough by pushing it away with palm of hand, pulling dough up with finger tips and folding dough back over. Repeat until dough is well mixed.

4. Refrigerate dough several hours until chilled.

5. Preheat oven to 350°F. On lightly floured surface, with rolling pin, roll half of dough ⅛" thick, keeping rest of dough refrigerated. Cut with 1" cookie cutter into desired shapes.

6. Arrange cookies about ½" apart on greased cookie sheets. Sprinkle with remaining sesame seeds, pressing seeds in gently. Bake until lightly browned, about 12 minutes. Cool cookies on racks.

* Vegetable shortening may be substituted for lard.

什錦水菓

WATERMELON SHELL FILLED WITH FRUIT

In summer when watermelon is in season, this is a most refreshing dessert to serve after a Chinese meal.

Serves 6 **Difficulty level 2**

1/2   **medium-sized watermelon**
1   **can (1 lb 4 oz) lychees***
1   **can (1 lb 4 oz) loquats***
1/4   **lb seedless green grapes**

1. Scoop melon with a melon baller into balls, leaving a layer of pulp inside the rind about ½" thick. Place melon balls in a large bowl. Scallop edge of watermelon shell.

2. Drain lychees and loquats, reserve syrup.

3. Add lychees, loquats, and grapes to melon balls. Pour some reserved syrup on fruits and mix gently. Spoon fruit into the melon shell. Chill until ready to serve.

* Other fruits such as cantaloupe or honeydew may be added to the mixture or substituted for lychees or loquats.

STEAMED CAKE

Few families in China have ovens. Instead, Chinese steam their breads and cakes. This cake resembles sponge cake. It is low in cholesterol because it contains no cream or butter. You may double the recipe. Eat one and freeze the other. Reheat in steamer over boiling water for 5-10 minutes until heated through.

Serves 8-10   **Difficulty level 2**

3	large eggs	1/4	tsp baking powder
1/3	cup cold water	1/4	cup sugar
1/2	tsp vanilla extract	1	tsp sparkling colored
1	cup flour		sugar (optional)

1. Separate eggs. Beat whites until stiff.

2. Beat yolks, slightly, with water and vanilla.

3. Sift flour and baking powder. Add sugar and sift again.

4. Line bottom and sides of 8" round pan with waxed paper.

5. Heat 1½"-2" of water in steamer or wok.

6. Mix flour mixture into egg yolk mixture.

7. Fold beaten egg whites into batter.

8. Pour batter into prepared pan. Rap pan sharply on the counter several times to remove large air bubbles.

9. With protective gloves, place pan on rack in steamer or wok over boiling water. Cover and steam over medium-high heat for 25 minutes, or until toothpick inserted in cake comes out clean. Remove cake from steamer.

10. To remove cake from pan, cover pan with a round plate and invert cake onto plate. Peel paper from bottom of cake. Turn cake over onto serving plate. Sprinkle top with colored sugar. Keep warm in steamer over low heat until ready to serve. Serve hot.

拔 丝 苹 果

SPUN APPLES

If you already make candy, this recipe will be easy for you. The temperature of the syrup is critical, so use a candy thermometer.

Serves 6-8   **Difficulty level 3**

1	cup flour
1	egg, beaten and mixed with 1/2 cup plus 2 TBS cold water
2	medium-sized firm apples
3	cups and 1 TBS salad oil
1	cup sugar
1/4	cup cold water
1	TBS black sesame seeds (optional)

1. Measure flour into medium-sized bowl. Pour egg mixture slowly over flour, stirring constantly until smooth.

2. Cut apples into quarters. Peel off skin and cut away cores. Cut each quarter lengthwise in half. Drop apple wedges into the batter; stir until coated.

3. Place oil, sugar, water, and sesame seeds near range. Spread oil lightly over a large serving plate. Into a large bowl, pour one quart of water; add a dozen ice cubes.

4. Heat 3 cups oil to 375°F in a 3-quart saucepan. Meanwhile, in a wok, over high heat, heat 1 tablespoon oil, sugar, and water to boiling, stirring only until sugar dissolves. Cook briskly, without stirring, until the syrup reaches 300°F on a candy thermometer, or turns a tea color, or hard crack stage (when a drop of syrup forms a hard mass in ice water). Stir in black sesame seeds. Reduce heat to its lowest point.

5. In hot oil, fry half of apple wedges at a time, until lightly browned. Drain on paper towel. Place wedges into hot syrup, stirring to coat thoroughly with syrup. Drop wedges, one at a time, into bowl of iced water. Syrup coating will harden instantly. Transfer spun apples to lightly greased serving plate. Serve immediately.

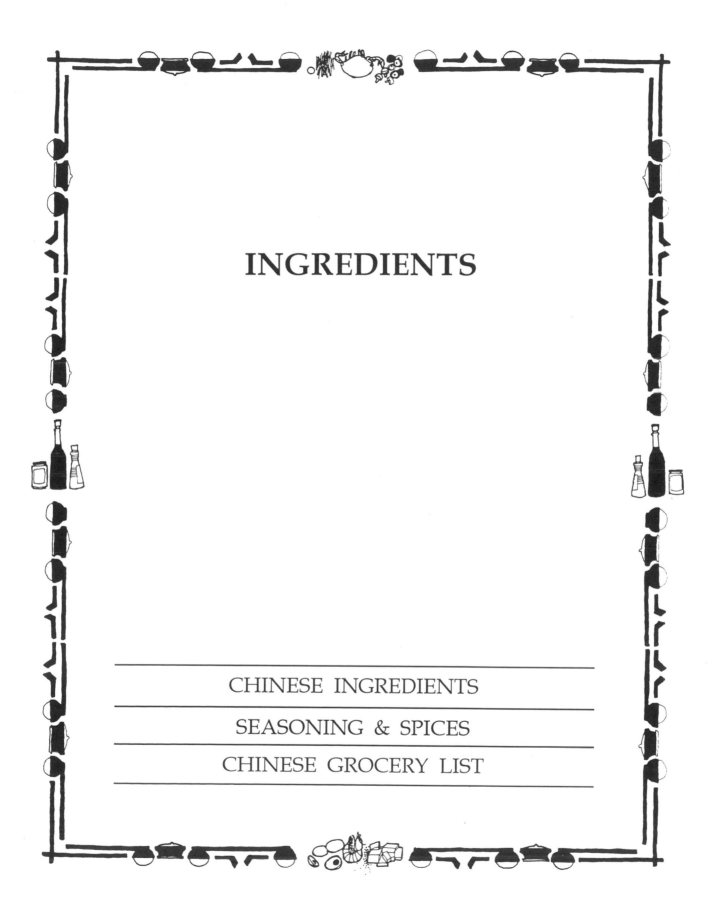

INGREDIENTS

CHINESE INGREDIENTS

SEASONING & SPICES

CHINESE GROCERY LIST

INGREDIENTS

CHINESE INGREDIENTS

All Chinese ingredients used in the recipes in this cookbook are listed in this chapter in alphabetical order. A brief description is given, plus information on how to use and store the ingredients.

When buying canned goods, check for dents and rust. Also check to see if the ends of the can are bulging. Spoiled foods produce gases that push out on the ends of the can. Do not attempt to open such cans, as you run the risk of having spoiled food splattered all over your kitchen. When in doubt, throw canned foods out rather than run the risk of suffering food poisoning. Vacuum sealed cans that do not hiss when opened should also be discarded.

For refrigerated items, check the expiration date if one is printed on the package. Select clean and undamaged packages. Do not buy bottles that are leaking or boxes with broken plastic wrap. Check each item carefully before purchasing.

Before storing dried Chinese ingredients, make sure the wrapping is not broken. Most imported food products from the Orient have been in ships and warehouses for a number of months. My mother always opened the imported packages and spread the contents on a tray. She placed them in the sun for a few hours during the hottest part of the day. I put mine on a tray in a low oven for an hour or so until they are dried. Another easy method is to place the packages in the freezer and freeze for 24 hours.

The recommended way to store Oriental dried foods is in covered glass jars. Empty peanut butter and mayonnaise jars are perfect for such purposes. First, wash jars thoroughly; then sterilize them in the dishwasher or in boiling water. For large, bulky dried foods, use large plastic bags with a seal or covered containers. These keep the food fresher longer.

✧　　　✧　　　✧

AGAR AGAR: A dried seaweed available in two forms. Threads resemble transparent noodles and are used for salad. Also sold in sheets and used in place of unflavored gelatin for desserts. For gelatin, soak in hot water until dissolved. For salad, soak 5-10 minutes in cold water to soften. Store dried, in sealed container at room temperature; keeps indefinitely.

ALMONDS: Raw, blanched, or toasted nuts. Use mainly as garnish for flavoring. To blanch, shell and soak 5 minutes in hot water. Rinse in cold water and slip off skin. To toast, heat 1 TBS salad oil in a skillet. Saute until golden. Store in airtight container at room temperature or freeze.

BAMBOO SHOOTS: Young, tender, ivory-colored vegetable shoots. Come in 2 varieties: winter and spring. Available canned and sometimes fresh. Canned, whole, tipped shoots packed in water are preferred. Adds texture and fiber to soups, seafood dishes, and vegetables. Rinse before using. Do not store in can. Refrigerate in covered container filled with water. Change water every other day. Keeps more than a week.

BEAN SPROUTS: Tender sprouts of mung beans. Available fresh or canned. Fresh sprouts are preferable. Blanch for salads, stir-fry with meat or other vegetables. Refrigerate in unsealed bag in vegetable drawer. Keeps only 2-3 days.

BEAN THREADS: Thin and translucent noodles made from mung beans. Often known as "Saifun," Chinese vermicelli, or cellophane noodles. Soften in warm water for 5-10 minutes. Do not overcook or threads will become gluey. Store at room temperature. Keeps for several months.

BOK CHOY: Tender, delicate vegetable with white stems and large green leaves. Often known as Chinese cabbage. Also available as baby Bok Choy. Can be stir-fried or cooked in soup. Too strong in flavor to be eaten raw. Refrigerate in unsealed bag in vegetable drawer. Keeps 4-5 days.

CABBAGE, CHINESE GREEN: 4"-5" long vegetable with green leaves and green stems, sold in bunches. Chinese name is "Sin Kan Sai," also known as "Heart of Cabbage," sometimes mistranslated as "baby Bok Choy." Frequently used in banquet dishes. Parboil before stir-frying. Refrigerate in unsealed bag in vegetable drawer. Keeps 4-5 days.

CABBAGE, NAPA: A crisp, tightly wrapped vegetable with firm, yellow-white leaves, tinted green at the edges. Has a distinctive but mild flavor. Also known as Chinese celery, lettuce, or cabbage. Use in soups and stir-fry dishes. Refrigerate in unsealed bag in vegetable drawer. Keeps more than a week.

CASHEWS: Raw or roasted nut in the shape of a kidney. Use mainly to garnish or to add a crunchy texture and nutty flavor. Store in airtight container at room temperature or freeze.

CILANTRO: Highly aromatic vegetable, has willowy stems and broad flat serrated leaves. Stronger and more distinctively flavored than parsley. In China, cilantro is called "Fragrant Green." Use as a garnish for soups and cold dishes. Wash, discard tough stems, chop leaves, or leave them whole. Refrigerate in a jar with the stems in water; cover with a plastic bag. Keeps 1-2 weeks.

CORN, BABY: Young, tender ear corn, about 2"-3" long, sold in cans and packed in water. Used most often for stir-frying. Drain before cooking. Refrigerate in covered container filled with cold water. Change water every other day. Keeps about one week.

DAIKON: Vegetable resembling large, white radish about 2" in diameter and 10"-15" long. Can substitute turnip or white radish for daikon. Use in soups and salads, also as a garnish on cold dishes. Peel, slice, or shred. Refrigerate in unsealed bag in vegetable drawer. Keeps over a week.

DUMPLING WRAPPERS: Small, thin, dough rounds made of flour and water. Sold in plastic packages in the refrigerated section of grocery store. Also known as Gyoza or Potsticker wrappers. Can be deep-fried or pan-fried. Refrigerate or freeze in sealed bag. Keeps about a week.

FUNGUS, BLACK: Small, dried, charred-looking fungus about 1" in size. Also known as "Cloud Ears" or "Wood Ears." Substitute for Chinese black mushrooms. Use in soups and stir-fry dishes. Often combined with golden needles. Must be soaked 5-10 minutes in hot water. Wash, rinse, and remove stems. Store in covered jar at room temperature. Keeps for months.

GOLDEN NEEDLES: Dried, elongated lily buds, about 2"-3" long. Pale golden in color. Have delicate, musky taste, high nutritive value. Also known as lily buds, lily flowers, or "Tiger Lilies." Use as a vegetable or flavoring. Must be soaked in hot water 5-10 minutes. Wash and drain well. Cut off stem and cut in half. Store in covered jar at room temperature. Keeps for several months.

JELLYFISH: Transparent, dehydrated marine animal. Sold in the refrigerated section of grocery stores. Available in sheets or shreds. Adds crispy texture to salads. Soak overnight in warm water. Rinse well. Refrigerate or freeze. Keeps for months.

LOQUATS: 1"-2" oval-shaped, peach-colored fruit, similar to apricot. Ripen in early spring. Also available in cans. Mainly served as dessert with lychees. To prepare fresh loquats, just peel and eat; discard brown seeds. Refrigerate leftover canned loquats in covered container. Keeps 4-5 days.

LYCHEES: Juicy, white, oval-shaped fruit with red, rough shell and hard brown seeds. Fresh only in July. Available in cans. Also known as lichees or lychee nuts. Use in desserts and in cooking. Eat fresh lychees as soon as possible. Refrigerate leftover, canned lychees in covered container. Keeps 4-5 days.

MUSHROOMS, BLACK: Dried black mushrooms from the Orient are meaty, succulent, and savory. The large, thick ones are the best and most expensive. Use in soups, also stir-fried, braised, or steamed dishes. Soak in warm water for 15 minutes. Cut off whole stem. Reserve liquid for stock. Store in airtight container in cool and dry place. Keeps for several months.

MUSHROOMS, GOLDEN: Pale yellow, thread-like mushrooms, 1"-1½" long. Tender and flavorful. Available fresh or canned. Also known as thread mushrooms. Use in soups, salads, and stir-fried dishes. Adds crunchy texture. Refrigerate in covered container. Keeps 2-3 days.

MUSHROOMS, STRAW: Smooth, grayish-brown mushrooms about 1" long. Available fresh or canned. Canned ones come peeled or unpeeled. Also known as grass mushrooms. May substitute champignon. Use in stir-fried dishes. Adds texture. Fresh ones deteriorate within 2-3 days. Refrigerate in unsealed bag in vegetable drawer. Drain canned ones; refrigerate in covered container filled with cold water. Change water every other day. Keeps for 4-5 days.

RICE STICKS: Made from rice pounded into flour. Come in many different widths. Choose medium-sized for deep-frying; they puff up better. Often known as Py-Mei-Fun meaning white rice noodles. Can be deep-fried and used as a garnish to add crunchy texture. Also used for stir-frying, but must be soaked first. Store in airtight container at room temperature. Keeps indefinitely.

SESAME SEEDS: Small, flattish seeds. Available in two varieties: black and white. Black sesame seeds are mainly used in desserts. White sesame seeds are used in salads and cooked dishes. Store at room temperature. Keeps indefinitely.

SNOW PEAS: Green vegetable, crisp in texture and sweet in taste. Also known as pea pods. Smaller pods are more tender than larger ones. Use in soups and stir-fried dishes. Snap off both ends of snow peas and remove strings from the sides. Wash and drain well. Refrigerate in unsealed bag in vegetable drawer. Keeps 4-5 days.

STRING BEANS: Yard-long beans are 1-3 feet in length. Similar to French beans; come in 2 colors, light and dark green. Only available from late spring to autumn. Use as a substitute for green beans. Use in stir-fry dishes, seasoned with garlic. Cut off stems and break into 2" pieces. Refrigerate in unsealed bag in vegetable drawer. Keeps for 2-3 days.

TOFU: See chapter on tofu (pages 150-151).

TOFU, BAKED SAVORY: Tofu that has been seasoned and baked. Comes as 4 brown-colored flat cakes wrapped in plastic. Sold in the refrigerated section of Oriental grocery stores. Can be eaten as is or cooked with vegetables and meat. Store in the coldest part of the refrigerator. Keeps 2-3 days. Can be frozen but the texture will become spongy.

TOFU SPAGHETTI: White, thin strips of pressed, fresh tofu. Sold in 6 oz. packages in the refrigerated section of Oriental grocery stores. Use in salads. Must be parboiled or soaked in boiling water for half an hour. Store in the coldest part of the refrigerator. Keeps 2-3 days.

TOFU STICKS: Pale yellow, dried bean curd sticks, about 20" long, folded in half. Sold in packages. Highly nutritious. Use in soups and stir-fried, braised, and stewed dishes. Must be soaked in boiling water for half an hour before using. Store in covered container at room temperature. Keeps for several months.

WATER CHESTNUTS: Dark brown bulbs, about the size of large walnuts. The nut inside is white and crunchy. Available sometimes fresh, most often in cans. Adds texture. Fresh water chestnuts must be refrigerated. Wash and peel before eating. Canned ones need to be drained and sliced. Refrigerate in plastic container filled with cold water. Change water every other day. Keeps more than a week.

WATERCRESS: Plant that grows in fresh water ponds. Composed of a stem with pungent or peppery leaves. Use in salads, soups, and as a garnish. Refrigerate in unsealed bag in vegetable drawer. Keeps 3-4 days.

SEASONINGS & SPICES

BEANS, FERMENTED BLACK: Small, soft, black preserved soybeans; have strong, pungent, and salty taste. Use as a seasoning, often with garlic, in seafood and meat dishes. Must be soaked in cold water for 5 minutes. Rinse and drain well. Store in airtight container at room temperature. Will keep indefinitely.

BEAN SAUCE, HOT: Hot and spicy paste made from soy beans. Available in cans or jars. Use as a seasoning, especially with bland foods like tofu. Unopened cans or jars may be stored at room temperature. Once opened, store in covered jar and keep in refrigerator. Will keep for several months.

CORNSTARCH: Powdered corn product. Sold in cardboard boxes in baking department. Use to thicken sauces, to glaze and bind food, and to seal in juices during cooking. Store at room temperature. Keeps indefinitely.

DRY SHERRY: A dry white wine with 17% alcohol. A substitute for Chinese rice wine. Avoid cooking or cream sherry, which have too much flavor. Use in eggs, meat, and all seafood dishes to remove strong odor. Keeps for months at room temperature.

FIVE SPICE POWDER: A group of spices—anise seed, cinnamon, licorice, clove, and ginger—ground together into a rich and flavorful powder. Use as a seasoning, especially for tofu dishes. Store at room temperature.

GARLIC: Pinkish-white, strong pungent flavor bulbs. Sold by weight. The larger the size, the milder the taste. Use mainly to season seafood, vegetables, and tofu. Store at room temperature or refrigerate in vegetable drawer. Keeps for several months.

GINGER: A beige-colored root with shiny skin. Pieces vary in size and shape. Sold by weight. Use to remove strong odors and add pungent flavor. Use the flat of cleaver to crush ginger before cooking. Refrigerate in vegetable drawer. Do not freeze. To keep indefinitely: wash, peel, and slice ginger. Refrigerate in covered jar filled with dry sherry.

GINGER JUICE: Juice made from fresh ginger. Two ways to make ginger juice: 1. Use a garlic press to extract juice from chopped ginger. 2. Soak 1 TBS shredded ginger in 1 TBS water for 10-15 minutes. Use in dishes that call for ginger flavor without the presence of minced ginger. Refrigerate in a covered container. Keeps for several days.

GREEN ONION: Green, thin, long leaves with white bulb and root. The smaller the bulbs, the milder the flavor. Also known as scallion. Use as accent, both in color and taste. Often used with ginger. Remove dying outer leaves, wash and cut off roots. Refrigerate in vegetable drawer, wrapped with paper towel, to keep dry. Do not store in sealed plastic bags. Keeps over a week.

KETCHUP: A condiment consisting of a thick, smooth-textured, spicy sauce made with tomatoes. The word ketchup comes from the Chinese: Koi = minced seafood, Tsai = sauce. Also known as tomato catsup. Use in seasoning seafood, also as a dip for deep-fried foods. Refrigerate after opening. Keeps for several months.

OIL, CHILI: Hot sauce made from small red chili peppers and salad oil. Sold in bottles. Use for cooking and as a dip. Use sparingly. Store at room temperature. Keeps indefinitely.

OIL, SALAD: Oil made from vegetable. The best types to use are odorless, tasteless, and clear, such as vegetable canola oil, corn oil, and peanut oil. Buy quality (brand name) for best results. Use for stir-frying and deep-frying. Store fresh oil in bottle at room temperature. Keeps indefinitely. Oil used for deep-frying may be reused 3-4 times. To remove odor from used oil, heat to 375°F, add 2-3 slices of fresh ginger or raw peeled potato. Strain well and refrigerate.

OIL, SESAME: Amber-colored oil made from toasted white sesame seeds. Strong, nut-like, aroma and fragrance. Use as a flavoring. Adds subtle taste to soups, salads, and stir-fried dishes. Store at room temperature. Becomes stale after 6 months and loses its fragrance.

OIL, VIRGIN OLIVE: Pale green oil from pressed olives. Has rich flavor depending on quality and price. Use in salads. Too strong for most Chinese cooking. Store at room temperature. Keeps indefinitely.

OYSTER SAUCE: A thick, brown sauce made from oysters cooked in soy sauce and brine. Makes food smooth, rich, subtle-flavored, and velvety textured. Sold in cans and bottles. Use in stir-fried or braised dishes. Gives accent to all kinds of food. Often used in Cantonese dishes. Store in bottle at room temperature. Keeps indefinitely.

PEPPER, DRY RED: Dried hot chili peppers sold in bags. The smaller the peppers, the hotter they are. Use as a seasoning. May be omitted in recipes if not fond of hot, spicy food. Cut away tips of pepper, chop, and remove all seeds. Wash hands afterwards. Do not touch eyes while working with peppers. Store in covered jar at room temperature. Keeps indefinitely.

SHRIMP, DRY: Small, salted, pink, shelled shrimp, about ½" in length. Available in packages. Use as a seasoning for mild flavored food, such as tofu and Chinese cabbage. Use as substitute for pork or ham in soup. Must be soaked in cold water for 15 minutes. Save liquid to use as stock. Store in covered jar at room temperature. Keeps for several months.

SOY SAUCE: Made from soybeans, flour, salt, water, and sunshine, if naturally brewed. Available in cans or bottles. There are 2 basic types: regular and dark. Regular soy sauce is used for general purposes. Dark soy sauce adds rich color to braised and stewed dishes. Low sodium or less salty soy sauce is also available. Use for seasoning or as a dip. Open bottle by cutting a thin slice off the top part of plastic with a knife, thus exposing 2 small holes. Cover holes with the cap when not in use. Store at room temperature. Keeps indefinitely.

STAR ANISE: Dry, small, brown-colored seed, shaped like an 8 point star. Sold in small packages. Substitute for anise seed. Like licorice, use for flavoring eggs and meat dishes. Store at room temperature. Keeps indefinitely.

SUGAR: A sweetener usually made from fruits and vegetables. Most recipes call for white refined sugar. Light brown sugar may add more flavor and sweetness. Chinese use sugar to balance the saltiness of soy sauce or salt. Store at room temperature. Keeps indefinitely.

SZECHUAN PEPPERCORN: A mildly hot spice with pleasant aroma. Looks like black peppercorn, but is brown in color and hollow inside with only one small seed. Very aromatic. Also known as Chinese peppercorn or brown peppercorn. Use as a seasoning. Stir-fried with salt and then coarsely ground, it becomes a dip for deep-fried foods (see recipe on Flavored Peppered Salt, page 64). Store at room temperature. Keeps indefinitely.

SZECHUAN PEPPERCORN POWDER: Powder made from Szechuan peppercorn. Sold in small jars. Substitute for Five Spice Powder. Use as a seasoning for stir-fried dishes and as a dip with salt. Store at room temperature. Keeps indefinitely.

VINEGAR, CIDER: Made from juice of apples, diluted with water and fermented. Mild in flavor and pale yellow in color. Sold in bottles. Use in salads and in sweet and sour sauces. Store at room temperature. Keeps for several months.

VINEGAR, RICE: Made of glutinous rice, water, and salt. Has aromatic taste. Available in white, red, and dark colors. The best brands are imported from China. Substitute for cider vinegar. White rice vinegar is used with sweet and sour dishes, red rice vinegar as a dip for broiled crab, black or dark vinegar with braised or stir-fried dishes and as a table condiment. Store at room temperature. Keeps for several months.

VINEGAR, WHITE: Made from sun-ripened grain, diluted with water. Has pungent taste. Use in pickling vegetables, also in salads and sweet and sour dishes. Excellent for cleaning the wok and tea kettle. Store at room temperature. Keeps for several months.

CHINESE GROCERY LIST

Take this list with you when shopping in Oriental grocery stores. This will help you to buy the right kinds of food without guessing. If you are unable to find a particular item, show the Chinese characters to a Chinese salesperson. I have included some brand names in parentheses to assist in identifying the products.

Chinese	English	Information
洋菜然	Agar Agar	Transparent threads for salad; sheets for dessert
杏仁	Almonds	Raw, blanched, or toasted
竹笋	Bamboo Shoots	Young tipped shoots canned in water are best (Wei-Chuan, Jack Pot)
辣豆瓣醬	Bean sauce or paste, hot	Canned or in a jar (Szechuan, Yeo's)
粉丝	Bean thread (Saifun)	Dried, 2 oz. pkg. is easiest to use (Lungkow, L & W)
豆豉	Beans, fermented black (salted black beans)	Soft to touch, sold in packages (Mee Chun)
白菜	Bok Choy	Smaller leaves with shorter stems are more tender
小白菜	Bok Choy, baby	White, tender stems with green leaves; sold in bundles
青剧菜	Cabbage, Chinese Green (Sin Kan Sai)	Sometimes mislabeled as baby bok choy; short, green stems are preferable
包心菜	Cabbage, Napa (Chinese celery)	Firm, tight, heavy heads are best
玉米笋	Corn, baby (young, sweet corn)	Canned in water (Jack Pot, Cal Island, Fortuna)
辣醬	Chili sauce or paste, hot	Small jars; some come with garlic (Lan Chi, Yang Shing)

Chinese	English	Information
水餃皮	Dumpling wrappers (Gyoza)	Round flour skins sold in refrigerated section (Dynasty, Golden Dragon)
春捲皮	Egg roll wrappers (spring roll)	Large, square flour skins sold in refrigerated section (Dynasty, Peking)
木耳	Fungus, Black (Cloud Ears, Wood Ears)	Medium-sized is best for stir-frying (Unicorn, Wong Pai)
薑	Ginger	Smooth and shiny skin is preferable; firm root pieces
金針	Golden Needles (lily buds, Tiger Lilies, dried cabbage)	Dried; light color in small packages is preferable (Golden Cock, L & W, Roxy)
火腿	Ham, Smithfield	Sold by the pound, or order from Virginia ham catalog
海蜇皮	Jellyfish	Packaged, in refrigerated section; sheets or shredded
枇杷	Loquats	Canned whole in heavy syrup (Wei-Chuan, Ma Ling)
荔枝	Lychees (Lichee nuts)	Canned whole in heavy syrup (Wei-Chuan, Twin Dragon)
冬菇	Mushrooms, Chinese black	Dried; the thicker and larger ones are more fragrant (Wong Pai)
香菇	Mushrooms, Golden (thread mushrooms)	Fresh or canned (Jack Pot, L & W)
草菇	Mushrooms, Straw (grass mushrooms)	Peeled or unpeeled, fresh or canned (L & W, Twin Dragon, Wei-Chuan)
芥末	Mustard, hot	Powdered form in jar is hotter than pre-mixed (Coleman's, S & B)
辣油	Oil, Chili	Bottled (Han How, Orchids)

Chinese	English	Information
麻油	Oil, sesame	Chinese style is more aromatic than other brands (Lian How, Hsin Tung Yang)
蠔油	Oyster sauce (oyster flavored sauce)	Imported bottles are preferable (Old Brand, Lee Kum Kee)
雪豆	Peas, snow (pea pods)	Smaller, greener peas are more tender
紅辣椒	Pepper, dry red (hot chili pepper)	Larger pepper is less hot; dried and packaged in cellophane
蘇梅醬	Plum sauce	Bottled or canned (Koon Chun)
米	Rice (long grain)	Fluffy and light (Uncle Ben's)
米	Rice (short grain)	Aromatic and sticky (Calrose, Kokuho)
白米粉	Rice sticks (Py-Mei-Fun)	Medium-sized sticks are preferable for deep-frying (Lee Cheung Woo, Sailing Boat)
芝蔴	Sesame seeds (black and white)	Cheaper in Oriental grocery stores; sold in packages
大茴香	Star anise cloves (dried aniseed)	3 oz. package, sold with dry goods
醬油	Soy sauce	Naturally brewed is best, bottled or canned
生抽	(regular)	(Superior Sauce, Kikkoman)
老抽	(dark)	(Soy Superior Sauce, Mushroom Sauce)
花椒	Szechuan Peppercorn	Small jar or package
花椒粉	Szechuan Peppercorn powder	Difficult to find; substitute for Five Spice Powder (Wind Mill)
紅茶	Tea, black (red tea)	Loose tea leaves sold in canister, foil, or box; may substitute for Oolong Tea (San Chai, A.B.C., China Lichee)

Chinese	English	Information
菊花茶	Tea, Chrysanthemum	Dried herbal flowers in packages (Mong Lee Shang, China Prod.)
青茶	Tea, green	Loose tea leaves sold in canister, foil, or box; smaller leaves are better (China National Native Prod., Best Tea)
香片茶	Tea, Jasmine	Loose tea leaves with jasmine flowers. Sold in canister, foil, or box (Sunflower, Ten Ren's)
烏龍茶	Tea, Oolong	Loose tea leaves sold in canister, foil, or box (Ten Ren's, Best Tea)
豆腐	Tofu (bean curd)	Check expiration date and firmness (Fuyama, AFC)
五香豆腐	Tofu, baked savory (baked bean curd cake)	The darker the color, the more flavorful; sold in refrigerated section (Wy Ky Food Prod., AFC)
豆腐然	Tofu spaghetti	6 oz. package, sold in refrigerated section (WyKy, AFC)
元枝腐竹	Tofu sticks (dried bean curd)	Dried sticks sold in packages (Lee Cheung Woo, AFC)
鎮江醋	Vinegar, Rice (brown vinegar)	Bottled in China is preferable (Chinkiang, Koon Chun)
馬蹄	Water chestnuts	Fresh or canned (Ma Lin, Dynasty, Twin Dragon)
馬蹄粉	Water chestnut starch (chestnut powder)	Chestnut powder in box (Chi Kong, Ma Lin)
餛飩皮	Wonton wrappers	Small, square flour skins, sold in refrigerated section (Dynasty, Golden Dragon)

RECIPE INDEX

Recipe Index (Continued)

INDEX

ABOUT THE AUTHOR

Lily Loh was featured by CNN-TV and her cooking class was taped for the "On The Menu" program. Lily also does food demonstrations for TV Channels 3 and 8. She has been interviewed by The San Diego Union, San Diego Tribune, North Coast Dispatch, Blade-Tribune, and San Diego Magazine. Her latest article was published in Lady's Circle Magazine entitled "Chinese Cooking with Lily Loh."

Lily was born in the cosmopolitan city of Shanghai, China. She has nine sisters and brothers. Her family always had a chef, who was well supervised by her vegetarian mother who loves to cook. Her mother-in-law, who is also a gourmet cook, helped her expand her culinary skills.

When Lily was 7 years old her family moved to Hong Kong, where she was introduced to delicious Cantonese seafood and Dim Sum. Lily also lived in Brazil for a few years before she came to the United States to study Home Economics. She received a B.S. from Purdue University and an M.A. from Cornell University, where she taught for several years.

Her love for teaching and cooking inspired her to start her own Chinese cooking school in California. She has been teaching since 1976. At present she has four different series of classes: Beginners, Advanced, Seafood and Vegetables, and Specialty (Dim Sum). She is now working on a fifth class called Quick Woking which is the subject of her newest TV show and her next cookbook. Her students include chefs, homemakers, professional people, teenagers, and cooking teachers. She also does food demonstrations for the Del Mar Fair and the San Diego Home/Garden Show.

Lily is a Certified Culinary Professional by the International Association of Culinary Professionals. She is a member of the Southern California Culinary Guild, the Home Economics Association, and Omicron Nu. Currently, Lily lives in Solana Beach, California, with her husband and two children. Besides cooking, teaching, and writing she still finds time to play bridge and tennis.